The Mind of God
& Other Musings

The Mind of God
& Other Musings
The Wisdom of Science

Selected and with
an Introduction
by
SHIRLEY A. JONES

THE CLASSIC WISDOM COLLECTION
NEW WORLD LIBRARY
SAN RAFAEL, CALIFORNIA

The Classic Wisdom Collection
Published by New World Library
58 Paul Drive, San Rafael, CA 94903

Cover design: Greg Wittrock
Cover photo: Ian Gatley, National Optical Astronomy
   Observatories
Text design: Nancy Benedict

Library of Congress Cataloging-in-Publication Data

The mind of God & other musings : the wisdom of science /
   selected and with an introduction by Shirley A. Jones.
      p. cm. — (The Classic wisdom collection)
   Includes bibliographical references (p. 131).
   ISBN 1-880032-48-1 (alk. paper)
   1. Science — Philosophy — Quotations, maxims, etc.
   2. God — Quotations, maxims, etc. 3. Knowledge,
   Theory of (Religion) — Quotations, maxims, etc.
   4. Philosophy, Modern — Quotations, maxims, etc.
   I. Jones, Shirley A., 1947– . II. Series.
   Q175.M6343 1994
   501—DC20   94-19589
                                                   CIP

ISBN 1-880032-48-1

Printed in the U.S.A. on acid-free paper
Distributed by Publishers Group West

10 9 8 7 6 5 4 3 2 1

"I want to know God's thoughts . . .
the rest are details."

ALBERT EINSTEIN

Contents

CONTENTS

Publisher's Preface

Life is an endless cycle of change. We and our world will never remain the same.

Every generation has difficulty relating to the previous generation; even the language changes. The child speaks a different language than the parent.

It seems almost miraculous, then, that certain voices, certain books, are able to speak to not only one, but many generations beyond them. The plays and poems of William Shakespeare are still relevant today — still capable of giving us goose bumps, still entertaining, disturbing, and profound. Shakespeare is the writer who, in the English language, defines the word classic.

There are many other writers and thinkers who, for a great many reasons, can be considered classic, for they withstand the test of time. We want to present the best of them to you in the New World Library Classic Wisdom Collection, the thinkers who, even though they lived many years ago, are still relevant and important in today's world for the enduring words of wisdom they created, words that should forever be kept in print.

In *The Mind of God and Other Musings — The Wisdom of Science,* editor Shirley A. Jones has pulled off a quiet miracle. Her collection of words of scientists through the years provides a profound and sparklingly clear reflection of our civilization, our science, our spiritual nature, and our place in the universe. Anyone who reads these words will be touched by them and, quite possibly, even changed by them, becoming a broader and deeper thinker and a more compassionate player in the endlessly fascinating game of life.

Marc Allen
New World Library

Introduction

We are all evolving together on a cosmic stage. This evolution is not the Darwinian kind that can be seen physically; it is the kind that is felt deep inside as the consciousness elevates.

Each generation opens that consciousness a crack more. We can see there is more to us than meets the eye.

The carbon in our tissues, the iron in our blood, and the calcium in our bones are all components of a universe that burst forth perhaps fifteen billion years ago. We are not just protoplasm; we are stardust. All our dust collectively brightens the planet we live on.

When we harmoniously complement one another, with the full knowledge that the actions of the microcosm affect those of the macrocosm, we lift our sights toward higher awareness and more thoughtful action. Complementing one another is the true nature of our relationship with the universe and with each other; and in the process, as we *compliment* one another in a spirit filled with acceptance and appreciation, we honor both our individuality and our unity.

We are all evolving in spirit: No matter what, we will evolve. Yet there are certain beings who seem to do it with an extra verve, a heightened heart that reaches the consciousness of all ages in time and mind. Spiritual leaders like Gautama Buddha and Jesus Christ, humanitarians like Abraham Lincoln and Martin Luther King Jr., and scientists like Benjamin Franklin and Albert Einstein exist as stellar examples.

The biologist Edmund W. Sinnott expressed his feeling about such individuals: "It is the living man, by the contagion not of his words alone but of his deeds and example, who through the ages has set other men ablaze and put in their hearts high aspirations. . . ."

That "contagion" — that extra verve — spreads throughout the pages of this book of thoughts. It is a collection of words from scientists dating from about 430 B.C. to the present. Not all the scientists are as famous as Einstein, but all are as human in their need to explore their common ground of being — as human as you or I.

As you read through these pages, you will find that their words shape themes. Universal truths, ageless and timeless, emerge. Curiously, or maybe not so curiously, these truths parallel those agreed upon by The Parliament of the World's Religion. When more than one hundred of the world's faiths — Confucianism, Judaism, Christianity, Islam, goddess worship, Bahaism, Buddhism to name a few — came together in September 1993, they had a singular purpose in mind: to come up with a cosmic script that protects and promotes the well-being of all humanity in the spirit of harmony.

Spiritual and scientific pursuits, historically on divergent paths, are now beginning to merge in this spirit of harmony. From The Parliament of the World's Religion, we hear the universal tenets:

1. We are interdependent.
2. We take individual responsibility for all we do.
3. We must treat others as we wish others to treat us.
4. We consider humankind our family.
5. We must strive for a just social and economic order, in which everyone has an equal chance of reaching his or her full potential.
6. We commit ourselves to a culture of respect, justice and peace.
7. Earth cannot be changed for the better unless the consciousness of individuals is changed first.

The introduction to the ten-page document closes with, "We commit ourselves to this global ethic, to understanding one another, and to socially beneficial, peace-fostering and nature-friendly ways of life. We invite all people, whether religious or not, to do the same."

This introduction invites you to do the same as you explore with Margaret Mead, Antonie van Leeuwenhoek, Louis Pasteur, Marie Curie, Stephen Hawking, Thomas Huxley, and nearly two hundred other scientists. In their own ways — funny, sad, and sage — they share the contagion of their words. They share not as people filled with wisdom, but as people seeking a unity of purpose — the same sought by religious leaders of the world.

Echoing this purpose, the themes of Cosmic Sense, Infinite Fields, Interlaced Patterns, Creative Expressions, The Great Architect, Enduring Patterns, The Spirit of Nature, Quest of Discovery, Bountiful Knowledge, True Axioms, Great Spans, and Future of Hope become your themes and the world's themes. They are not mutually exclusive categories; they weave in and out of one another, creating a purposeful design.

Presented in practical, yet often poetic, prose and grounded in experience, the words of this spirited cast of scientists touch the sensitivities of those seeking the wholeness of the science of life, the cosmic picture. You can see these scientists not just in their roles of biologist, anthropologist, physicist, astronomer, zoologist, or ecologist; you can also see them as fellow seekers who live in a world full of questions, curiosities, hopes, and fears.

These wisdom seekers are people who have earned their living and our respect by stepping beyond conventional thoughts. Sometimes rewarded, sometimes persecuted, they search, generation after generation, for ways to connect the seemingly diverse parts of life to the whole of living.

Their desire to open their minds — and their hearts — guides them in their quest of discovery, not always in comfort, but always in anticipation and always with a consciousness ready to stretch higher and brighter.

We, as fellow discoverers, can appreciate that stretch — the big one that reaches from the calcium in our bones to the hydrogen atoms in our stars. We can feel, and know, the awe of this connection as we stretch the awareness of ourselves and our environment to include the whole cosmic stage of possibilities and perceptions. As the physicist Niels Bohr puts it, "We are both spectators and actors in the great drama of existence."

The wisdom collected in this volume directs us

to a place on center stage where we can spread the contagion of our high aspirations and feel the excitement and energy of the entire cast and audience around us — a place where we can experience this fine production called life, continuously in production, creatively evolving.

Shirley A. Jones
Stockton, California, 1994

1

The Universe

COSMIC SENSE

The ultimate stuff of the universe is mind stuff.

SIR ARTHUR EDDINGTON (1882–1944)
BRITISH THEORETICAL ASTRONOMER

The existence of a Being endowed with intelligence and wisdom is a necessary inference from a study of celestial mechanics.

SIR ISAAC NEWTON (1642–1727)
BRITISH PHYSICIST

That deeply emotional conviction of the presence of a superior reasoning power, which is revealed in the incomprehensible universe, forms my idea of God.

ALBERT EINSTEIN (1879–1955)
SWISS-AMERICAN PHYSICIST

To get a universe that has expanded as long as ours has without either collapsing or having its matter coast away would have required extraordinary fine-tuning.

MICHAEL TURNER (B. 1927), U.S. PHYSICIST

Something deeply hidden had to be behind things.

ALBERT EINSTEIN (1879–1955)
SWISS-AMERICAN PHYSICIST

The universe can be best pictured, though still very imperfectly and inadequately, as consisting of pure thought, the thought of what we must describe as a mathematical thinker. . . . If the universe is a universe of thought, then its creation must have been an act of thought.

SIR JAMES JEANS (1877–1946)
BRITISH ASTRONOMER

The most beautiful system of the Sun, planets, and comets could only proceed from the counsel and dominion of an intelligent and powerful Being.

SIR ISAAC NEWTON (1642–1727)
BRITISH PHYSICIST

A planet may in a very real sense be said to have a life of its own, of which what we call life may or may not be a detail. It is born, has its fiery youth, its sober middle age, its palsied senility, and ends at last in cold incapability of further change, its death.

PERCIVAL LOWELL (1855–1916)
U.S. ASTRONOMER

The planets inevitably become individuals to any one who learns to know them during the long, quiet nights in the country. . . . Like individuals of whatever kind, they impress different persons in different ways. As I have watched them from year to year, I have come to have a very distinct impression of Jupiter as slow and majestic, and yet not lacking in joviality; Saturn as friendly, but reserved; Mars as sturdily brisk and busy; Venus as always gracious and smiling; and Mercury as irresponsible and roguish. . . . An intimate acquaintance with them, which is not wholly scientific, cannot fail to stamp them as in some sort individuals. . . . To know about the planets is to know about ourselves.

MARTHA EVANS MARTIN (D. 1925)
U.S. ASTRONOMER

It makes no sense to say the universe has no sense.

NIELS BOHR (1885–1962), DANISH PHYSICIST

THE COSMIC CODE

I passionately believe in a universe with purpose, though I cannot prove it.

OWEN GINGERICH (B. 1930)
U.S. ASTROPHYSICIST

I think the universe is a message written in code, a cosmic code, and the scientist's job is to decipher that code.

HEINZ R. PAGELS (B. 1939)
U.S. PHYSICIST

The effort to understand the universe is one of the very few things that lifts human life a little above the level of farce, and gives it some of the grace of tragedy.

STEVEN WEINBERG (B. 1933), U.S. PHYSICIST

What is the universe? Is it a great 3-D movie in which we are all unwilling actors? Is it a cosmic joke, a giant computer, a work of art by a Supreme Being, or simply an experiment? The problem in trying to understand the universe is that we have nothing to compare it with.

HEINZ R. PAGELS (B. 1939), U.S. PHYSICIST

He who gazes at the stars unavoidably starts thinking.

GERHARD STAGUHN (B. 1952), U.S. PHYSICIST

Man comes into a universe so vast, cold, and in-scrutable that in it he feels utterly lost and insignifi-cant — "a stranger and afraid, in a world he never made." The price he pays for reason is to be sur-rounded with problems that he cannot solve, with mysteries that seem unfathomable. In this cosmic darkness the little candle that is life is a comforting reminder that there is stirring here the germ of something like himself, something that can grow into a bright light on his course to show him the di-rection that he ought to take.

EDMUND W. SINNOTT (1888–1968)
U.S. BIOLOGIST

Our common-sense experience and our evolutionary history have prepared us to understand something of the workaday world. When we go into other realms, however, common sense and ordinary intuition turn out to be highly unreliable guides.

CARL SAGAN (B. 1934), U.S. ASTRONOMER

Ideas come from space.

THOMAS ALVA EDISON (1847–1931)
U.S. SCIENTIST

Now, my suspicion is that the universe is not only queerer than we suppose, but queerer than we can suppose. . . . I suspect that there are more things in heaven and earth than are dreamed of, in any philosophy.

J. B. S. HALDANE (1892–1964)
BRITISH GENETICIST

You will never be able to see inside a blackhole, and you can never know what has happened inside, since no energy in any form ever comes out to carry the information. We call it "cosmic censorship."

KIP S. THORNE (B. 1940), U.S. ASTRONOMER

There is no center holding anywhere, as far as we can see, and we can see great distances. What we thought to be the great law of physics turns out to be local ordinances, subject to revision any day.

LEWIS THOMAS (1913–1993), U.S. BIOLOGIST

Astronomy is thus a four-legged animal standing on sound and false ideas at the front and false observations at the rear. Amazingly the beast can limp forward, sometimes even gallop, from one discovery to the next.

STEPHEN JAY GOULD (B. 1941)
U.S. GEOLOGIST–PALEONTOLOGIST

We are spreading the light of reason out across the universe.

RICCARDO GIACCONI (B. 1931)
U.S. ASTRONOMER

Philosophy is written in this grand book — I mean the universe — which stands continually open to our gaze, but it cannot be understood unless one first learns to comprehend the language and interpret the characters in which it is written.

GALILEO GALILEI (1564–1642)
ITALIAN PHYSICIST-ASTRONOMER

The recent tendencies of science do, I believe, take us to the eminence from which we can look down into the deep waters of philosophy; and if I rashly plunge into them, it is not because I have confidence in my powers of swimming, but to try to show that the water is really deep.

SIR ARTHUR EDDINGTON (1882–1944)
BRITISH THEORETICAL ASTRONOMER

The concept of an instrument that can look to the far reaches of the universe and say something about what it means to be human — that touches everyone. It's an incredibly romantic idea.

STORY MUSGRAVE (B. 1935), U.S. ASTRONAUT

I can see my footprint in the moon like fine grainy particles.

NEIL ARMSTRONG (B. 1930), U.S. ASTRONAUT

The universe seems to possess a "structure," and our judgments of aesthetic and moral values result from the degree of spiritual sensitivity our living systems have to what this structure is.

EDMUND W. SINNOTT (1888–1968), U.S. BIOLOGIST

The eventual goal of science is to provide a single theory that describes the whole universe. . . .

STEPHEN HAWKING (B. 1942)
BRITISH THEORETICAL PHYSICIST

Considered in its concrete reality, the stuff of the universe cannot divide itself but, as a kind of gigantic atom, it forms in its totality the only real indivisible.

PIERRE TEILHARD DE CHARDIN (1881–1955)
JESUIT PALEONTOLOGIST

All places are alike . . . in the universe.

ALBERT EINSTEIN (1879–1955)
SWISS-AMERICAN PHYSICIST

THE SLANT OF THE SUN

Life is a pure flame, and we live by an invisible Sun within us.

SIR THOMAS BROWNE (1605–1682)
BRITISH MEDICAL RESEARCHER

There is nothing of a physical nature that is more friendly to man, or more necessary to his well-being, than the sun. From the sun you and I get every bit of our energy, the chemical energy, energy that gives life and sustains life; that builds skyscrapers, and churches; that writes poems and symphonies. In its rays is the magic stuff of life itself.

DAVID E. LILIENTHAL, CHAIRMAN
U.S. ATOMIC ENERGY COMMISSION, 1947–1950

The celestial fire which flows to us on the earth from the Sun is not such a fire as there is in heaven, neither is it like that which exists upon the earth, but the celestial fire with us is cold and congealed, and it is the body of the Sun.

THEOPHRASTUS PARACELSUS (1493–1541)
SWISS ALCHEMIST

As if seated upon a royal throne, the Sun rules the family of the planets as they circle round him.

NICOLAUS COPERNICUS (1473–1543)
POLISH ASTRONOMER

The sun, with all those planets revolving around it and dependent upon it, can still ripen a bunch of grapes as if it had nothing else in the universe to do.

GALILEO GALILEI (1564–1642)
ITALIAN PHYSICIST-ASTRONOMER

Relative to Earth, the Sun is a gigantic thermal power plant; relative to the Milky Way it is a tiny luminous point of medium brightness that would be hard to find in the outer arms of the spiral. And this point of light is circled by a blue speck, a million times smaller, on which a very strange species roams of late, regarding itself as very big and important.

GERHARD STAGUHN (B. 1952), U.S. PHYSICIST

Keep in the sunlight.

BENJAMIN FRANKLIN (1706–1790)
U.S. SCIENTIST

INFINITE FIELDS

To cross our own galaxy from side to side would take not less than ten million years . . . and yet, on a cosmic scale, the distance across the galaxy is hardly any distance at all.

FRANCIS CRICK (B. 1916), BRITISH BIOPHYSICIST

I see a picture of a universe that becomes infinite. It can expand and expand and expand until it is sufficiently thinly spaced to allow another universe to begin. And that perhaps surrounding our universe is the far, faint remnant of another universe; and beyond that, of another one, even fainter, and so on, infinitely.

ISAAC ASIMOV (1920–1992), U.S. BIOCHEMIST

Who as a child did not lie in bed filled with a slowly mounting terror while sinking into the idea of a universe that goes on and on, forever and ever?

RUDY RUCKER (B. 1946), U.S. RESEARCHER

A sunbeam, setting out through space at the rate of 186,000 miles a second would, in this universe, describe a great cosmic circle and return to its source after a little more than 200 billion terrestial years.

LINCOLN BARNETT (1907–1970)
SCIENCE WRITER

Let us in imagination board some miraculous sky-ship. . . . We arrive at Jupiter in fifty-five years after we left the sun; at Saturn in 101 years; at Uranus in 203 years; and at Neptune in 318 years. If we should continue to distant and inconspicuous Pluto, we should arrive there in 420 years. And yet at the rate of our travel we could eat breakfast in New York, luncheon in London, and return to New York for dinner and the theater. . . .

FOREST RAY MOULTON (1872–1952)
U.S. ASTRONOMER

Whenever man tries to probe into the universe's dimension of time, he will finally be confronted with eternity. Where he tries to understand the dimension of space, he will be finally confronted with infinity. And where he tries to understand matter by separating it into ever smaller particles, he will always discover something that is even smaller, and be confronted with the fact that there is no final smallest particle.

GERHARD STAGUHN (B. 1952)
U.S. PHYSICIST

Six specks of dust inside Waterloo Station represent
— or rather over-represent — the extent to which
space is crowded with stars.

SIR JAMES JEANS (1877–1946)
BRITISH ASTRONOMER

But it is said that outside of the heavens there is no
body, nor place, nor empty space, in fact, that nothing
at all exists, and that, therefore, there is no space in
which the heavens could expand; then it is really
strange that something could be enclosed by nothing.

NICOLAUS COPERNICUS (1473–1543)
POLISH ASTRONOMER

The earth . . . lies right in the middle of the heavens.

CLAUDIUS PTOLEMAEUS (PTOLEMY)
(2ND CENTURY A.D.), EGYPTIAN ASTRONOMER

When I consider the small span of my life absorbed
in the eternity of all time, or the small part of space
which I can touch or see engulfed by the infinite im-
mensity of spaces that I know not and that know me
not, I am frightened and astonished to see myself
here instead of there . . . now instead of then.

BLAISE PASCAL (1623–1662), FRENCH PHYSICIST

MATTER OF POSSIBILITIES

That our planet is the one and only planet where life
has emerged would be a ridiculous assumption. . . .
Even if only one in a hundred of the ten billion suit-
able planets has actually got life well under way,

there would be more than 100 million such planets. No, it is presumptuous to think that we are alone.

HARLOW SHAPLEY (1885–1972)
U.S. ASTRONOMER

If they be not inhabited, what a waste of space!

NATIONAL GEOGRAPHIC (MAY 1974)
"THE INCREDIBLE UNIVERSE," ANONYMOUS

Perhaps there do exist universes interpenetrating with ours; perhaps of a high complexity, perhaps containing their own forms of awareness. . . . It is not the physicist's job to make this sort of speculation, but today, when we are so much less sure of the natural world than we were two decades ago, he can at least license it.

D. H. WILKINSON (B. 1922)
BRITISH NUCLEAR PHYSICIST

The greatest thing that could happen to me would be for creatures to come from space and pick me up and take me away. . . . This is a matter of possibilities. . . . The possibilities are absolutely immense. It's one chance in a billion I'd succeed in making contact, but what have I got to lose?

STORY MUSGRAVE (B. 1935), U.S. ASTRONAUT

The proof that objects of planetary size do exist outside the solar system indicates that our planets are not unique and uncommon anymore. The evidence is such that there is no need to question the reality of this.

ALEXANDER WOLSZCZAN (EXPRESSED: 1994)
U.S. ASTRONOMER

2

Connections

INTERLACED PATTERNS

For the seeds and universal elements of the world are so interlaced in sundry ways, and mingled one within another. . . .

PLINY THE ELDER (23–70 A.D.)
ROMAN NATURALIST

Every grain of sand, every tip of a leaf, even an atom contains the entire universe. Conversely, the universe can be perceived as the tip of a leaf.

GERHARD STAGUHN (B. 1952), U.S. PHYSICIST

What pattern connects the crab to the lobster and the orchid to the primrose and all four of them to me? And me to you?

GREGORY BATESON (1904–1980)
U.S. ANTHROPOLOGIST

My parents, Gregory Bateson and Margaret Mead, were scientists and teachers. . . . The minds of both sought patterns of completeness, wholes, and so they thought of worlds entire, whether these worlds were minute images of microscopic life within a drop of water or the planet wreathed in cloud. They thought of worlds and drew me into them.

MARY CATHERINE BATESON (B. 1939)
U.S. ANTHROPOLOGIST

It is usually not recognized that for every injurious or parasitic microbe there are dozens of beneficial ones. Without the latter, there would be no bread to eat nor wine to drink, no fertile soils and no potable waters, no clothing and no sanitation. . . . They keep in constant circulation the chemical elements which are so essential to the continuation of plant and animal life.

SELMAN A. WAKSMAN (1888–1973)
"FATHER OF ANTIBIOTICS"

The logical structure of science is analogous to a spider's web. Start anywhere on the web and work inward, and eventually you come to the same core. Understanding this core of knowledge, then, is what science is all about.

ROBERT M. HAZEN (B. 1948)
U.S. GEOPHYSICAL SCIENTIST

The first mistake is to think of mankind as a thing in itself. It isn't. It is part of an intricate web of life. And we can't think even of life as a thing in itself. It isn't. It is part of the intricate structure of a planet bathed by energy from the Sun.

ISAAC ASIMOV (1920–1992), U.S. BIOCHEMIST

The farther and more deeply we penetrate into matter, by means of increasingly powerful methods, the more we are confounded by the interdependence of its parts. . . . It is impossible to cut into the network, to isolate a portion without it becoming frayed and unravelled at all its edges.

PIERRE TEILHARD DE CHARDIN (1881–1955)
JESUIT PALEONTOLOGIST

GROUNDED IN UNITY

Every part of an element separated from its mass desires to return to it by the shortest way.

LEONARDO DA VINCI (1452–1519)
ITALIAN SCIENTIST AND ARTIST

A single man has not nearly the value he would have in a state of union. He is an incomplete animal. He resembles the odd half of a pair of scissors.

BENJAMIN FRANKLIN (1706–1790), U.S. SCIENTIST

We pass the word around; we ponder how the case is put by different people; we read the poetry; we meditate over the literature; we play the music; we change our minds; we reach an understanding. Society evolves this way, not by shouting each other down, but by the unique capacity of unique, individual human beings to comprehend each other.

LEWIS THOMAS (1913–1993), U.S. BIOLOGIST

I have a fantasy. What if we had a president who said, "I want the members of my cabinet to be committed to actually talking to each other about the problems that they have to face, and to start from the premise that those problems are interconnected. . . ." If you had that attitude, you'd save a lot of money, because what we do now is break all the problems up in pieces. Everyone has a totally separate bureaucracy, stepping on each other's toes, and leaving out things that need to be attended to.

MARY CATHERINE BATESON (B. 1939)
U.S. ANTHROPOLOGIST

A few weeks ago I received a letter from a magazine editor inviting me to join six other people at dinner to make a list of the Seven Wonders of the Modern World. . . . I had to look up the old, biodegradable Wonders, the Hanging Gardens of Babylon and all the rest, and then I had to look up the word "wonder" to make sure I understood what it meant. It then occurred to me that if the magazine could get any seven people to agree on a list of any such seven things you'd have the modern Seven Wonders right there at the dinner table.

LEWIS THOMAS (1913–1993), U.S. BIOLOGIST

I learned that a definition of panic is a state of unrelatedness.

HORTENSE POWDERMAKER (1896–1970)
U.S. ANTHROPOLOGIST

One of the things that you get from being trained as an anthropologist is experience in thinking about the whole . . . that family life, and how we make a living, and how our religious beliefs are developing, and how our government institutions function — that all of these things are interconnected, and that we can't really solve major problems without thinking in terms of all these different areas.

MARY CATHERINE BATESON (B. 1939)
U.S. ANTHROPOLOGIST

Slightly less embarrassing than owning to a philosophy of life is confessing that you have some idea, though vague and changing, as to what constitutes the good life. My ideas of it come chiefly from a comparison between civilization and primitive culture. . . . On the basis of my years with the Stone Age Eskimos I feel that the chief factor in their happiness was they were living according to the Golden Rule. . . . Man is more fundamentally a co-operative animal than a competitive animal. His survival as a species has been perhaps through mutual aid rather than through rugged individualism. And somehow it has been ground into us by the forces of evolution to be "instinctively" happiest over those things which in the long run yield the greatest good to the greatest number.

VILHAJALMUR STEFANSSON (1879–1962)
ANTHROPOLOGIST

As the traveler who has once been from home is wiser than he who has never left his own doorstep, so a knowledge of one other culture should sharpen our ability to scrutinize more steadily, to appreciate more lovingly, our own.

MARGARET MEAD (1901–1978)
U.S. ANTHROPOLOGIST

We often visited Ellen's homeland, where our children had no trouble becoming attached to the Danish scene. When I asked our son how he could communicate with the Danish children with whom he played, he said, "We can't talk together, but we can laugh together."

VICTOR WEISSKOPF (B. 1908)
AUSTRIAN-AMERICAN PHYSICIST

No amount of knowledge of the culture of one group will take us very far. There must be an equally technical analysis of the other group involved in the interaction. To get along with the French we must understand ourselves as well as the French.

S. L. WASHBURN (B. 1911)
U.S. ANTHROPOLOGIST

All human beings on Earth, however different they may appear superficially, are essentially alike. Humanity today forms a single species.

ISAAC ASIMOV (1920–1992), U.S. BIOCHEMIST

What is human and the same about the males and females classified as Homo sapiens is much greater than the differences.

ESTELLE R. RAMEY (B. 1917), U.S. PHYSIOLOGIST

The male form of a female liberationist is a male liberationist — a man who realizes the unfairness of having to work all his life to support a wife and children so that someday his widow may live in comfort, a man who points out that commuting to a job he doesn't like is just as oppressive as his wife's imprisonment in a suburb, a man who rejects his exclusion, by society and most women, from participation in childbirth and the engrossing, delightful care of young children — a man, in fact, who wants to relate himself to people and the world around him as a person.

MARGARET MEAD (1901–1978)
U.S. ANTHROPOLOGIST

Male and female have the power to fuse into one solid, because both are nourished in both and because

soul is the same thing in all living creatures, although the body of each is different.

HIPPOCRATES (460–400 B.C.)
GREEK, "FATHER OF MEDICINE"

A human being is part of the whole called by us a universe — a part limited in time and space. He experiences himself, his thoughts and his feelings, as
something separate from the rest, a kind of optical
delusion of his consciousness. This delusion is a kind
of prison for us; it restricts us to our personal deci-
sions and our affections to a few persons nearest to us.
Our task must be to free ourselves from this prison
by widening our circle of compassion to embrace all
living creatures and the whole of nature in its beauty.

ALBERT EINSTEIN (1879–1955)
SWISS-AMERICAN PHYSICIST

How far you go in life depends on your being tender
with the young, compassionate with the aged, sym-
pathetic with the striving, and tolerant of the weak
and strong because, in life, you will be all of these.

GEORGE WASHINGTON CARVER (1864–1943)
U.S. AGRICULTURAL SCIENTIST

Just concentrate on helping one person, giving hope
to one person, and that person in turn may give hope
to somebody else and it will spread out.

AARON ABRAHAMSEN (B. 1921)
U.S. AERONAUTICAL SCIENTIST

It has well been said that the organism is not an ag-
gregate but an integrate.

EDMUND W. SINNOTT (1888–1968)
U.S. BIOLOGIST

Man is slightly nearer to the atom than to the star. . . .

From his central position man can survey the grandest works of Nature with the astronomer, or the minutest works with the physicist.

SIR ARTHUR EDDINGTON (1882–1944)
BRITISH THEORETICAL ASTRONOMER

If matter and energy and chance are all there is, it takes a man of most unusual courage to build an unselfish love for humanity on such foundations. . . . Biology in its deepest sense stretches from cell to psyche.

EDMUND W. SINNOTT (1888–1968)
U.S. BIOLOGIST

Different as the planets are as individuals, they have too many characteristics in common to admit any question of their common origin. They are not simply stars of one sort and another that happen to lie nearer to us than the great body of stars that spangle the heavens, but are, without doubt, all of one family with us in their origin, as well as in their situation.

MARTHA EVANS MARTIN (D. 1925)
U.S. ASTRONOMER

We did not arrive on this planet as aliens. Humanity is part of nature. . . . The more closely we identify ourselves with the rest of life, the more quickly we will be able to . . . acquire the knowledge on which an enduring ethic, a sense of preferred direction, can be built.

EDWARD O. WILSON (B. 1929), U.S. BIOLOGIST

That's something I'm going to do throughout the spacewalks. I'm going to be sure to take moments, even though they're fleeting, to simply stop in my tracks and look at Earth or whatever's out there and think what this is all about. You've got to stop and do that . . . for humanity.

STORY MUSGRAVE (B. 1935), U.S. ASTRONAUT

There was, we remind ourselves, no atmosphere for the flag to wave in. . . . To be able to look at the American flag and know how much so many people had put of themselves and their work into getting it where it was . . . we sensed — we really did — this almost mystical identification of all the people in the world at that instant.

EDWIN EUGENE (BUZZ) ALDRIN (B. 1930)
U.S. ASTRONAUT

If astronomy teaches anything, it teaches that man is but a detail in the evolution of the universe. . . . He learns that though he will probably never find his double anywhere, he is destined to discover any number of cousins scattered through space.

PERCIVAL LOWELL (1855–1916)
U.S. ASTRONOMER

CAUSE AND EFFECT

The world is indeed only a small tide pool; disturb one part and the rest is threatened.

GREGORY BATESON (1904–1980)
U.S. ANTHROPOLOGIST

The least movement is of importance to all nature. The entire ocean is affected by a pebble.

BLAISE PASCAL (1623–1662), FRENCH PHYSICIST

I look with respect at the green "scum" on stagnant water and at slimy "water weeds" waving in a stream, for not only have they survived with little change through all the climatic and geologic modifications since the days when the earth was surfaced only with water and barren igneous rock, but their forebears gave rise to all the plant forms that have grown or still grow on the earth. If higher life as we know it were suddenly to vanish, these humble algae might still live on to start a new life cycle.

HELEN HOOVER (1910–1984)
U.S. METALLURGIST

The mixture of waves which constitutes sunlight has to struggle through the obstacles it meets in the atmosphere, just as the mixture of waves at the seaside has to struggle past the columns of the pier. . . . The long waves which constitute red light are hardly affected, but the short waves which constitute blue light are scattered in all directions. . . . A wave of blue light may be scattered by a dust particle, and turned out of its course. After a time a second dust particle again turns it out of its course, and so on, until finally it enters our eyes by a path as zigzag as that of a flash of lightning . . . the blue waves of the sunlight enter our eyes from all directions. And that is why the sky looks blue.

SIR JAMES JEANS (1877–1946)
BRITISH ASTRONOMER

Light, in the latest theory, is not waves in a sea of ether, or a jet from a nozzle; it could be compared rather to a machine gun fire, every photo-electric bullet of energy traveling in regular rhythm. . . . As each bullet hits an electron of chlorophyll it sets it to vibrating. . . . One electron is knocked galley west into a dervish dance like the madness of the atoms in the sun. The energy splits open chlorophyll molecules, recombines their atoms, and lies there, dormant, in foods.

DONALD CULROSS PEATTIE (1898–1964)
U.S. BIOLOGIST-NATURALIST

If you see a single blood cell in my veins and follow it, it will drift along; you won't be able to predict anything. But if you study the body as a whole, you might say, "I injured my finger and now my immune system is reacting." There's a global response to the injury and this is why this blood cell goes there. It's quite evident to me that the movement and development of one part is part of the pattern of organization of the larger system. In that sense I can see a purpose.

FRITJOF CAPRA (B. 1939), U.S. PHYSICIST

3

Creativity

IMAGINATION

Imagination disposes of everything; it creates beauty, justice, and happiness, which are everything in this world.

BLAISE PASCAL (1623–1662), FRENCH PHYSICIST

Imagination is more powerful than knowledge.

ALBERT EINSTEIN (1879–1955)
SWISS-AMERICAN PHYSICIAN

Newton's passage from a falling apple to a falling moon was an act of the prepared imagination.

JOHN TYNDALL (1820–1893), IRISH PHYSICIST

An act of imagination, a speculative adventure . . . underlies every improvement of natural knowledge.

SIR PETER BRIAN MEDAWAR (1915–1987)
BRITISH ZOOLOGIST

My spirit was with other things. I turned the chair to the fireplace and sank into a half sleep. The atoms flitted before my eyes. Long rows, variously, more closely, united; all in movement wriggling and turning like snakes. And see, what was that? One of the snakes seized its own tail and the image whirled scornfully before my eyes. As though from a flash of lightning I awoke; I occupied the rest of the night in working out the consequences of the hypothesis. . . . Let us learn to dream. . . .

(FRIEDRICH) AUGUST KEKULÉ (1829–1896)
GERMAN CHEMIST (MOLECULAR STRUCTURE
OF BENZENE, A CLOSED CARBON RING)

Every tool carries with it the spirit by which it has been created.

WERNER KARL HEISENBERG (1901–1976)
GERMAN PHYSICIST

The modern physicist and anyone who would understand what he is up to, must therefore learn to work in two worlds. One is a world of brass and glass and wax and mercury and coils and lenses and vacuum pumps . . . the other is a world of visualization and creative imagination. . . .

EDWARD U. CONDON (1902–1974), U.S. PHYSICIST

In early days the habit was such that on going to bed, it was a source of satisfaction to me to think I should be able to lie for a length of time and dwell on the fancies which at the time occupied me; and frequently next morning, on awakening, I was vexed with myself because I had gone to sleep before I had revelled in my imaginations as much as I had intended.

HERBERT SPENCER (1820–1903)
BRITISH ANTHROPOLOGIST

They're big . . . and they're gone. . . . I think dinosaurs fill a really important niche. They allow us to use our imagination.

JACK HORNER (B. 1946), U.S. PALEONTOLOGIST

THE MYSTERIOUS

As long as we do science, some things will always remain unexplained.

FRITJOF CAPRA (B. 1939), U.S. PHYSICIST

The most beautiful experience we can have is the
mysterious. . . . He to whom this emotion is a
stranger, who can no longer pause to wonder and
stand rapt in awe, is as good as dead. . . .

ALBERT EINSTEIN (1879–1955)
SWISS-AMERICAN PHYSICIST

You look out at the sky, and you look at Jupiter. It
brings in all of us the same wonder, the same awe
about the universe. I think the astronomer has more
awe and wonder because he knows what it is that is
up there. His knowledge doesn't diminish his awe; it
enhances it.

MAXINE SINGER (B. 1931), U.S. GENETICIST

We do not understand much of anything, from . . .
the "big bang," all the way down to the particles in
the atoms of a bacterial cell. We have a wilderness of
mystery to make our way through in the centuries
ahead.

LEWIS THOMAS (1913–1993), U.S. BIOLOGIST

I was and still am puzzled by the fact that the wind
blows preferably from the west in our latitudes. Once
I asked a famous meteorologist for an explanation.
He asked me to come to his office, where he showed

me his computer outputs calculating the wind directions, taking into account the solar radiation, the ro-
tation of the earth, and other important facts. "You
see," he said, "all the arrows in the middle latitudes
point west to east." I replied, "Now the computer un-
derstands it, but what about you and me?"

VICTOR WEISSKOPF (B. 1908)
AUSTRIAN-AMERICAN PHYSICIST

If we want to solve a problem that we have never
solved before, we must leave the door to the unknown ajar.

RICHARD P. FEYNMAN (1918–1988)
U.S. PHYSICIST

Man can learn nothing unless he proceeds from the
known to the unknown.

CLAUDE BERNARD (1813–1878)
FRENCH PHYSIOLOGIST

Do not become a mere recorder of facts, but try to
penetrate the mystery of their origin.

IVAN PETROVICH PAVLOV (1849–1936)
RUSSIAN PHYSIOLOGIST

I like being outside, I like digging holes in the
ground, I like the mystery. When I find something, I
still get just as excited as I did at first.

JACK HORNER (B. 1946), U.S. PALEONTOLOGIST

The zest, the fire, the savor of existence comes from
something deeper, something spontaneous, native,
and protoplasmic, which we can never outgrow or
avoid, not should we wish to do so.

EDMUND W. SINNOTT (1888–1968)
U.S. BIOLOGIST

It is enough for me to contemplate the mystery of conscious life perpetuating itself through all eternity, which we dimly perceive, and to try humbly to comprehend even an infinitesimal part of the intelligence manifested in nature.

ALBERT EINSTEIN (1879–1955)
SWISS-AMERICAN PHYSICIST

CREATIVE EXPRESSIONS

When a man undertakes to create something, he establishes a new heaven, as it were, and from it the work that he desires to create flows into him.

THEOPHRASTUS PARACELSUS (1493–1541)
SWISS ALCHEMIST

The ignition point at which interest will take fire to make the warmth of purpose is often so high that we cannot by ourselves generate the necessary heat to accomplish it. Desire and aspiration come oftener from something outside us, from the ideas and personalities of others.

EDMUND W. SINNOTT (1888–1968)
U.S. BIOLOGIST

Something very special sometimes happens to women when they know they will not have a child — or any more children. It can happen to women who have never married when they reach the menopause. It can happen to widows with children who feel that no new person can ever take the place of a loved husband. It can happen to young wives who discover they never can bear a child. Suddenly, their whole creativity is released — they paint or write as never

before or they throw themselves into academic work
with enthusiasm, where before they had only half a
mind to spare for it. . . .

MARGARET MEAD (1901–1978)
U.S. ANTHROPOLOGIST

If a man were deprived of sexual fulfillment and the
nobler enjoyments arising therefrom, all poetry, and
probably all moral tendency, would be eliminated
from his life.

BARON RICHARD VON KRAFFT-EBING (1840–1902)
GERMAN NEUROLOGIST

Shelley roundly declared that "poetry comprehends
all science," thus classifying scientific creativity with
the form of creativity. . . .

SIR PETER BRIAN MEDAWAR (1915–1987)
BRITISH ZOOLOGIST

The value of science remains unsung by singers, so
you are reduced to hearing — not a song or a poem,
but an evening lecture about it.

RICHARD P. FEYNMAN (1918–1988)
U.S PHYSICIST

I have often wondered why music was such an essential part of my life. . . . I cannot live constantly in the
scientific realm. I need the change to other approaches offered by music and the other arts. There is a saying, "In the morning I turn from mystery to reality,
in the evening I return from reality to mystery." We
need such differing approaches — Niels Bohr's com-
plementarity — as we sometimes need to turn to the
other side in bed in order to get comfortable.

VICTOR WEISSKOPF (B. 1908)
AUSTRIAN-AMERICAN PHYSICIST

In this momentous question as to the nature and quality of life we should not limit ourselves to an approach through science only, important as this is. The philosopher, the poet, the artist, and the mystic should all contribute their insights here, for all are concerned with life.

EDMUND W. SINNOTT (1888–1968)
U.S. BIOLOGIST

This indeed is man's creative gift, to find or make a likeness where none was seen before — a likeness between mass and energy, a link between time and space, an echo of all our fears in the passion of Othello.

JACOB BRONOWSKI (1908–1974)
BRITISH SCIENTIST

Science is one of the grand human activities. It uses the same kind of talent and creativity as painting pictures and making sculptures. It's not really very different, except that you do it from a base of technical knowledge.

MAXINE SINGER (B. 1931), U.S. GENETICIST

I believe that the scientist is trying to express absolute truth and the artist absolute beauty, so that I find in science and art, and in an attempt to lead a good life, all the religion that I want.

J. B. S. HALDANE (1892–1964)
BRITISH GENETICIST

Men seem not to be pushed into the finest things they do but to follow the urgent call of something that draws them on through hardship and uncertainty and discouragement to the attainment of a high desire.

EDMUND W. SINNOTT (1888–1968)
U.S. BIOLOGIST

It should not be hard for you to stop sometimes and look into the stains of walls, or ashes of a fire, or clouds, or mud or like place in which . . . you may find really marvelous ideas.

LEONARDO DA VINCI (1452–1519)
ITALIAN SCIENTIST-ARTIST

MYTHS AND MYSTICISM

Angels are probably destined to remain spiritual, and winged horses like Pegasus are likely to be forever myths; but biologists do not consider them impossible. Instead, they are put into another realm: they are highly improbable biological phenomena. Improbable biological phenomena cannot easily be pieced together by Nature from any of the mechanisms in her crowded cupboard of organismic machinery.

MICHAEL J. KATZ (B. 1928), U.S. BIOLOGIST

Before modern science there was ample room in the real world not only for natural events, but also for . . . supernatural ones alongside — there was a place for magic.

BERT HANSEN (B. 1922), U.S. SCIENTIST

I was in Safed with the Israeli mathematician Chaim Pekeris. Safed — now called Sfad — is the center of Jewish mysticism and the place where Rabbi Isaac ben Solomon Luria, an eminent interpreter of the Cabala, is buried. . . . Unfortunately, we happened to have been in Safed on a Saturday, when it is forbidden by tradition to visit a cemetery. But since this was the only day I could visit the rabbi's grave, we decided to go anyway. Luckily, the cemetery was not locked. In order to show our respect, and perhaps because we thought it might generally improve the situation, Pekeris and I wore yarmulkes (skullcaps) when we ascended the hill to the tomb. . . . Suddenly as we walked toward the grave we felt a gust of wind, and my yarmulke was blown away. We searched for twenty minutes and couldn't find it. We were both a little shaken, and Pekeris asked me whether we should proceed to the tomb. I said that we should — as scientists we shouldn't believe in such signs. We went to the tomb and on our way back searched again for the yarmulke, but in vain. It had miraculously vanished in the wind. . . . Mystical and psychic experiences should be considered complementary to the scientific approach.

VICTOR WEISSKOPF (B. 1908)
AUSTRIAN-AMERICAN PHYSICIST

Matter doubtless holds more possibilities than we can dream of now.

EDMUND W. SINNOTT (1888–1968), U.S. BIOLOGIST

In ancient and medieval times, gross or tangible matter was supposed to shade away through increasingly subtle grades of matter, like mists, smokes, exhalations, and air, to ether, animal spirits, the soul, and spiritual beings, all forming links in an essential unity.

JOHN READ (1884–1963), BRITISH CHEMIST

Warts can be ordered off the skin by hypnotic suggestion. Generations of internists and dermatologists, and their grandmothers, for that matter, have been convinced of the phenomenon.

LEWIS THOMAS (1913–1993), U.S. BIOLOGIST

The characteristic feature of mysticism is the breaking down of distinctions. Obviously, this is not an
unqualified good. If I can't tell my hand from my
sandwich, then I may bite myself. Opposed to the
human tendency towards mysticism we have rationality. Too much rationality quickly becomes inane
and boring. What is needed is some kind of bridge
between the two.

RUDY RUCKER (B. 1946)
U.S. MATHEMATICAL SCIENTIST

QUESTIONS AND CURIOSITIES

Science is not an inhuman or superhuman activity.
It's something that humans invented, and it speaks to
one of our great needs — to understand the world
around us. In the end, it makes you wonder whether
people have lost their curiosity, because that's all it is.

MAXINE SINGER (B. 1931), U.S. GENETICIST

Those who do not stop asking silly questions become
scientists.

LEON LEDERMAN (B. 1922)
U.S. NUCLEAR PHYSICIST

Ask questions. Don't be afraid to appear stupid. The
stupid questions are usually the best and the hardest
to answer. They force the speaker to think about the
basic problem.

PAUL EHRENFEST (1880–1933)
AUSTRIAN PHYSICIST

It would seem to me ... an offense against nature,
for us to come on the same scene endowed as we are

with the curiosity, filled to overbrimming as we are with questions, and naturally talented as we are for the asking of clear questions, and then for us to do nothing about or, worse, to try to suppress the questions. . . .

LEWIS THOMAS (1913–1993), U.S. BIOLOGIST

That man Leeuwenhoek was like a puppy who sniffs — with a totally impolite disregard of discrimination — at every object of the world around him!

PAUL DE KRUIF (1890–1971)
SCIENCE RESEARCHER

I regard myself in a way as a teacher, keeping alive certain vital questions about what makes a human life worthwhile, what is a good community, what is the human good. . . . These are the questions that really bother the young, and if you provide them with the opportunity to think about these things, and if you give them the books that will raise those questions most profoundly, the little candle might stay lit. . . .

MARY CATHERINE BATESON (B. 1939)
U.S. ANTHROPOLOGIST

The important thing is not to stop questioning. Curiosity has its own reason for existing. One cannot help but be in awe when he contemplates the mysteries of eternity, of life, of the marvelous structure of reality. It is enough if one tries merely to comprehend a little of this mystery every day. Never lose a holy curiosity.

ALBERT EINSTEIN (1879–1955)
SWISS-AMERICAN PHYSICIST

4

Spirituality

THE GREAT ARCHITECT

How did life originate? . . . We actually know so little about how life began that much time is required for repeating and repeating our own uncertainties. This was not always true. I knew in my boyhood on a back-country Indiana farm that life had been created by a kindly, very wise, so-capable "Mr. Jehovah," and that was that.

WARDER CLYDE ALLEE (1885–1955)
U.S. ZOOLOGIST

If there was a big bang the universe must have consisted of an infinite amount of energy concentrated in a single point. God knows where that came from.

GERHARD STAGUHN (B. 1952), U.S. PHYSICIST

I find no difficulty in imagining that, at some former period, this universe was not in existence, and that it made its appearance in consequence of the volition of some pre-existing Being.

THOMAS H. HUXLEY (1825–1895)
BRITISH BIOLOGIST

God in the beginning formed matter in solid massy, hard, impenetrable moving particles. . . .

SIR ISAAC NEWTON (1642–1727)
BRITISH PHYSICIST

The longer I live, the more convincing proofs I see of this truth, that God governs in the affairs of man; and if a sparrow cannot fall to the ground without his notice, is it probable that an empire can rise without his aid?

BENJAMIN FRANKLIN (1706–1790)
U.S. SCIENTIST

Great is God our Lord. Great is his power, and there is no end to his wisdom. Praise Him, you heaven, and glorify Him sun and moon, and you planets, for out of Him, through Him, and in Him are all things — every perception and every knowledge.

JOHANNES KEPLER (1571–1630)
GERMAN ASTRONOMER

What really interests me is whether God had any choice in the creation of the world.

ALBERT EINSTEIN (1879–1955)
SWISS-AMERICAN PHYSICIST

The idea of a universal and beneficent Creator does not seem to arise in the mind of man, until he has been elevated by long-continued culture.

CHARLES DARWIN (1809–1882)
BRITISH BIOLOGIST

I will frankly tell you that my experience in pro-longed scientific investigations convinces me that a belief in God — a god who is behind and within the chaos of vanishing points of human knowledge —

adds a wonderful stimulus to the man who attempts to penetrate into the regions of the unknown.

J. LOUIS R. AGASSIZ (1807–1873)
SWISS-AMERICAN ZOOLOGIST

God, the creator of the universe, can never be against learning the laws of what he has created.

MUSTAFA MAHMOUD
EGYPTIAN MEDICAL RESEARCHER

The very fact that the universe is creative, and that the laws have permitted complex structures to emerge and develop to the point of consciousness — in other words, that the universe has organized its own self-awareness — is for me powerful evidence that there is "something going on" behind it all.

PAUL DAVIES (B. 1946)
BRITISH PHYSICIST

In ultimate analysis, the universe can be nothing less than the progressive manifestation of God.

J. B. S. HALDANE (1892–1964)
BRITISH GENETICIST

BELIEF AND BELIEFS

The great error of the doctrines on the spirit has been the idea that by isolating the spiritual life from all the rest, by suspending it in space as high as possible above the earth, they were placing it beyond attack, as if they were not thereby simply exposing it to be taken as an effect of mirage! Just what the relation is of spirit of the body on the one hand, and to the universe on the other, is a problem we cannot solve; but to see the spirit as born in life, whatever its source or however lofty its final destiny may be, is a conception that helps draw it down out of the clouds and brings it closer to us.

EDMUND W. SINNOTT (1888–1968)
U.S. BIOLOGIST

Any effort to visualize God reveals a surprising childishness. We can no more conceive Him than we can conceive an electron.

LECOMTE DU NOUY (1849–1919)
FRENCH SCIENTIST

Nothing in life is more wonderful than faith — the one great moving force which we can neither weigh in the balance nor test in the crucible.

SIR WILLIAM OSLER (1849–1919)
CANADIAN RESEARCH SCIENTIST

When we pray, we link ourselves with the inexhaustible power that spins the universe.

ALEXIS CARREL (1873–1944)
FRENCH RESEARCH SCIENTIST

There are those — and I am one of them — who rebel at having to deal with an intermediary. They want to go to the fountain-head. Someone who knows me well says that science, to me, has been a religious experience. He is probably right. If my religious passion had been turned towards the Catholic Church I should have wanted to be a priest. . . . I have always been in direct touch with the fountain-head . . . my source of inspiration has always been direct.

CECILIA PAYNE GAPOSCHKIN (1900–1979)
BRITISH ASTRONOMER

My deeply held belief is that if a god of anything like

the traditional sort exists, our curiosity and intelligence is provided by such a God. We would be unappreciative of that gift ... if we suppressed our passion to explore the universe and ourselves.

CARL SAGAN (B. 1934), U.S. ASTRONOMER

The undevout astronomer is mad!

SIR WILLIAM HERSCHEL (1738–1822)
BRITISH ASTRONOMER

One truth stands firm. All that happens in world history rests on something spiritual. If the spiritual is strong, it creates world history. If it is weak, it suffers world history.

ALBERT SCHWEITZER (1875–1965)
ALSATIAN-BORN MEDICAL MISSIONARY

If religion has given birth to all that is essential in society, it is because the idea of society is the soul of religion.

EMILE DURKHEIM (1858–1917)
FRENCH ANTHROPOLOGIST

Many have quarreled about religion that never practiced it.

BENJAMIN FRANKLIN (1706–1790)
U.S. SCIENTIST

In my most extreme fluctuations I have never been an atheist in the sense of denying the existence of God.

CHARLES DARWIN (1809–1882)
BRITISH BIOLOGIST

God may forgive your sins, but your nervous system won't.

ALFRED KORZYBSKI (1879–1950)
POLISH-AMERICAN SCIENTIST

God is a living Being, eternal, most good; and therefore life and a continuous external existence belong to God, for that is what God is.

ARISTOTLE (384–322 B.C.)
GREEK PHILOSOPHER-SCIENTIST

Live innocently; God is here.

CAROLUS LINNAEUS (1707–1778)
SWEDISH BOTANIST

When I was four years old, my father died suddenly. . . . For the rest of my childhood I felt I was not like other children, for I had *two* fathers in heaven.

CECILIA PAYNE GAPOSCHKIN (1900–1979)
BRITISH ASTRONOMER

Conceiving God to be the fountain of wisdom, I thought it right and necessary to solicit his assistance for obtaining it; to this end I formed the following little prayer, which was prefixed to my tables of examination for daily use: "O powerful Goodness! bountiful Father! merciful Guide! Increase in me that wisdom which discovers my truest interest. Strengthen my resolution to perform what that wisdom dictates. Accept my kind offices to Thy other children as the only return in my power for Thy continual favors to me."

BENJAMIN FRANKLIN (1706–1790)
U.S. SCIENTIST

If America is to grow great we must stop gagging at the word "spiritual."

LAURENCE M. GOULD (B. 1896)
U.S. SCIENTIST AND MEDICAL RESEARCHER

THE TWAIN MEET

The person who thinks there can be any real conflict between science and religion must be either very young in science or very ignorant in religion.

JOSEPH HENRY (1797–1878), U.S. PHYSICIST

The fact that scientific method seems to reduce God to something like an ethical code may throw some light on the nature of scientific method; I doubt if it throws much light on the nature of God.

SIR ARTHUR EDDINGTON (1882–1944)
BRITISH THEORETICAL ASTRONOMER

Science was used to sap the base of religion. Science must be used to consolidate it.

LECOMTE DU NOUY (1849–1919)
FRENCH SCIENTIST

The biology of the human spirit will not be easy to investigate, because experience rather than experiment is such an important part of it, and for its full development there may be required some tools that science does not now possess.

EDMUND W. SINNOTT (1888–1968)
U.S. BIOLOGIST

In some sense the hydrogen atom, in the inseparability of its spirit and matter aspects, in its simplicity and complexity, in its relation to small whole numbers (and in other ways), is an image of the Self . . . a material reflection of God.

JOHN L. HITCHCOCK (B. 1936), U.S. PHYSICIST

One equation involves Planck's constant (h), the velocity of light (c), and the electronic charge (e). The combination hc/e happens to equal 137. . . . This number connects quantum theory (h), relativity (c), and electricity (e). Therefore, it holds a special significance for physicists. When I mentioned this number — 137 — to [Gershom] Scholem, his eyes popped out. . . . He told me that in Hebrew each letter of the alphabet has a numerical equivalent and that the Cabala assigned a deep symbolic significance to the sums of such numbers in a given word. The number corresponding to the word cabala happens to be 137. Could there be a connection between Jewish mysticism and theoretical physics?

VICTOR WEISSKOPF (B. 1908)
AUSTRIAN-AMERICAN PHYSICIST

I maintain that cosmic religious feeling is the strongest and noblest incitement to scientific research.

ALBERT EINSTEIN (1879–1955)
SWISS-AMERICAN PHYSICIST

If God exists He must be manifest somehow in matter. . . .

EDMUND W. SINNOTT (1888–1968)
U.S. BIOLOGIST

Quarks are located in a physical "somewhere" between matter and spirit. . . . The "inconceivable concept" of the electron as a "wave of matter" alone touches upon a metaphysical dimension. . . . These "waves of matter" are more than shape; they are metashape, shapes to which we can no longer attribute a substantial content — only a spiritual one.

GERHARD STAGUHN (B. 1952), U.S. PHYSICIST

The worldview now emerging from modern science is an ecological view, and ecological awareness at its deepest level is spiritual or religious awareness.

FRITJOF CAPRA (B. 1939), U.S. PHYSICIST

Science without religion is lame, religion without science is blind.

ALBERT EINSTEIN (1879–1955)
SWISS-AMERICAN PHYSICIST

Science ever has been, and ever must be, the safe-
guard of religion.

SIR DAVID BREWSTER (1781–1868)
SCOTTISH PHYSICIST

Whether in the intellectual pursuits of science or in
the mystical pursuits of the spirit, the light beckons
ahead and the purpose surging in our natures responds.

SIR ARTHUR EDDINGTON (1882–1944)
BRITISH THEORETICAL ASTRONOMER

BEYOND AND AGAIN

My mind is incapable of conceiving such a thing as a
soul. I may be in error, and man may have a soul; but
I simply do not believe it.

THOMAS ALVA EDISON (1847–1931)
U.S. SCIENTIST

We are spirits. That bodies should be lent us, while
they can afford us pleasure, assist us in acquiring
knowledge, or in doing good to our fellow creatures,
is a kind and benevolent act of God.

BENJAMIN FRANKLIN (1706–1790)
U.S. SCIENTIST

In the elderly and in children, the soul is bigger than
the body. It's only the rest of us who let our bodies
outgrow our souls.

ELISABETH KUBLER-ROSS (B. 1926)
U.S. MEDICAL RESEARCHER

You could take all the chemicals in the human body,
and you could put them together in some certain
ways, but they wouldn't add up to the powers that do
what living things do. . . . There's no way in the
world that you can begin to talk about those powers

in terms of objectified body. For that reason, this very classical notion of soul is useful.

MARY CATHERINE BATESON (B. 1939)
U.S. ANTHROPOLOGIST

The important point is that man's spirit, certainly an inhabitant of his living, material body, may without philosophical impropriety be regarded as similar in nature to a far greater Spirit, in which thus, literally, he may be said to live and move and have his being.

EDMUND W. SINNOTT (1888–1968)
U.S. BIOLOGIST

I often dream about falling . . . lately I dreamed I was clutching at the face of a rock but it would not hold. Gravel gave way. I grasped for a shrub, but it pulled loose, and in cold terror I fell into the abyss. Suddenly . . . a feeling of pleasure overcame me. I realized that what I embody, the principle of life, cannot be destroyed. . . . As I continued to fall in the dark void, embraced by the vault of the heavens, I sang to the beauty of the stars and made my peace with the darkness.

HEINZ R. PAGELS (B. 1939), U.S. PHYSICIST

The function of the human, rational soul is the noblest function of all, for it is itself the noblest of spirits. . . . Its gaze being turned towards the higher world, it loves not this lower abode and meaner station. . . . Its function is to wait for the revelation of truths.

AVICENNA (IBN SINA) (980–1037)
PERSIAN SCIENTIST

You seem solicitous about that pretty thing called Soul. I do protest you I know nothing of it: nor

whether it is, nor what it is, nor what it shall be. . . .
Let it be what it will, I assure you my soul has a great
regard for your own.

FRANCOIS-MARIE AROUET (VOLTAIRE) (1694–1778)
FRENCH SCIENTIST

I've never met a healthy person who worried much
about his health, or a good person who worried much
about his soul.

J. B. S. HALDANE (1892–1964)
BRITISH GENETICIST

The man who is always worrying whether or not his
soul would be damned generally has a soul that isn't
worth a damn.

OLIVER WENDELL HOLMES (1809–1894)
U.S. PHYSICIAN, RESEARCHER

As for a future life, every man must judge for himself between conflicting vague probabilities.

CHARLES DARWIN (1809–1882)
BRITISH BIOLOGIST

How many lives a person has lived is not nearly as
important as what you have done with them, what
have you gained. Personally, I would not be proud
finding out I had made 500,000 lives; I would be
ashamed of myself. I should be somewhere else.

AARON ABRAHAMSEN (B. 1921)
U.S. AERONAUTICAL SCIENTIST

I need heart *and* physics, but I believe that when I
die, I die, and it will be finished.

STEPHEN HAWKING (B. 1942)
BRITISH THEORETICAL PHYSICIST

If man's spirit is a part of that eternal Spirit in the universe, death may not exercise dominion over it. Just as it drew dead matter together to form the living body, so it may quit the body again and return to that unseen bourn from whence it came.

EDMUND W. SINNOTT (1888–1968)
U.S. BIOLOGIST

The body of Benjamin Franklin, Printer (like the cover of an old book, its contents torn out and stripped of its lettering and gilding), lies here, food for worms; but the work shall not be lost, for it will (as he believed) appear once more in a new and more elegant edition, revised and corrected by the Author.

BENJAMIN FRANKLIN (1706–1790), U.S. SCIENTIST
(EPITAPH COMPOSED FOR HIMSELF, 1728)

It is very beautiful over there.

THOMAS ALVA EDISON (1847–1931)
U.S. SCIENTIST
(PURPORTED LAST WORDS SPOKEN)

5

The Natural World

A LIVING, LIVELY SYSTEM

You cannot have a sparse planet any more than you can have half an animal.

JAMES LOVELOCK (B. 1919), U.S. SCIENTIST

How many species of organisms are there on Earth? The number could be close to 10 million or as high as 100 million. . . . It is a myth that scientists break out champagne when a new species is discovered. . . . We don't have time to describe more than a small fraction of those pouring in each year.

EDWARD O. WILSON (B. 1929), U.S. BIOLOGIST

By contrast with the emptiness of space, the living world is crammed with detail at every level. . . . For example, a drop of water contains rather more than a thousand billion billion water molecules.

FRANCIS CRICK (B. 1916), BRITISH BIOPHYSICIST

It is obvious that microbiologists will not run out of work for a couple of centuries.

JOSTEIN GOKSOYR (B. 1922)
NORWEGIAN MICROBIOLOGIST

Living beings form a special realm of science, filled with eye-popping collages of butterflies, sheets of grasses, mildewing molds, people, bears, whales and bats, eggs and embryos, grandmothers and grandfathers. Biology is about life, and life is organisms. . . . Afternoons poking about the Woods Hole seashore among horseshoe crabs, the seaweed, and the unicates or munching blue-eyed scallops and beach peas . . . or chipping ornate brachiopods from the shale . . . make me hesitate to think that I could ever dream of a creature that might not creep out from among the cattails one windy spring morning.

MICHAEL J. KATZ (B. 1928), U.S. BIOLOGIST

Nature is an infinite sphere whose center is everywhere and whose circumference is nowhere.

BLAISE PASCAL (1623–1662)
FRENCH PHYSICIST

It is interesting to contemplate an entangled bank, clothed with many plants of many kinds, with birds singing on the bushes, with various insects flitting about, and with worms crawling through the damp earth, and to reflect that these elaborately constructed forms, so different from each other . . . have all been produced by laws acting around us.

CHARLES DARWIN (1809–1882)
BRITISH BIOLOGIST

I have diverse pregnant and effectual reasons inducing me to believe that all water creatures breathe each one after their manner, as Nature hath ordained. . . .

PLINY THE ELDER (23–70 A.D.)
ROMAN NATURALIST

In one pool, on the right side of the path, is a family

of otters; on the other side, a family of beavers. . . . I was transfixed. As I now recall it, there was only one sensation in my head: pure elation mixed with amazement at such perfection. . . . I wished for no news about the physiology of their breathing, the co-ordination of their muscles, their vision, their endocrine systems, their digestive tracts. I hoped never to have to think of them as collections of cells. All I asked for was the full hairy complexity, then in front of my eyes, of whole, intact beavers and otters in motion.

LEWIS THOMAS (1913–1993), U.S. BIOLOGIST

I think that the novelty of nature is such that its variety will be infinite — not just in changing forms but in the profundity of insight and the newness of ideas. . . .

ISIDOR ISAAC RABI (1898–1988)
AUSTRIAN-AMERICAN PHYSICIST

The science of life is a superb and dazzlingly lighted hall which may be reached only by passing through a long and ghastly kitchen.

CLAUDE BERNARD (1813–1878)
FRENCH PHYSIOLOGIST

Life lives on life — it is cruel, but it is God's will.

ANTONIE VAN LEEUWENHOEK (1632–1723)
DUTCH MICROBIOLOGIST

I love to think of nature as an unlimited broadcasting station, through which God speaks to us every hour, if we will only tune in.

GEORGE WASHINGTON CARVER (1864–1943)
AGRICULTURAL SCIENTIST

Everything in the desert either stings, stabs, stinks or sticks. You will find the flora here as venomous, hooked, barbed, thorny, prickly, needled, saw-toothed, hairy, stickered, mean, bitter, sharp, wiry and fierce as the animals.

EDWARD ABBEY (1927–1989)
U.S. ENVIRONMENTALIST

The heart of animals is the foundation of their life, the sovereign of everything within them, the sun of their microcosm.

WILLIAM HARVEY (1578–1657)
BRITISH ANATOMIST

I can imagine no terminal point of human inquiry into nature, ever.

LEWIS THOMAS (1913–1993), U.S. BIOLOGIST

I escaped by myself to the river along one of our favorite paths with its tangled vines and bushes, its mistletoe-laden elms, its Cardinals, orioles, and gnat-catchers, its display of wayside flowers ... the exquisite great white prickly poppy, the rosin weeds, golden prionopsis, weedy horse nettle, and fierce tread-softly with its coarse spotted leaves. A large hawk flew to shelter in some cottonwoods pursued by six kingbirds and a dashing Scissor-tailed Flycatcher. One of the kingbirds was so excited that he attacked an inoffensive Turkey Vulture.... Under the great elms and cottonwoods on the river bank I watched the turbulent Canadian River and dreamed. The glory of nature possessed me. I saw that for many years I had lost my way. I had been led astray on false trails and had been trying to do things contrary to my nature. I resolved to return to my childhood vision of studying nature and trying to protect the wild things of the earth.

MARGARET MORSE NICE (1883–1974)
U.S. ORNITHOLOGIST

If a tree dies, plant another in its place.

CAROLUS LINNAEUS (1707–1778)
SWEDISH BOTANIST

ENDURING PATTERNS

It's nasty, damaged stuff. We know from chemical experiments that it degrades and how fast it degrades. After 25 million years, there shouldn't be any DNA left at all.

REBECCA CANN (EXPRESSED: 1993)
U.S. MOLECULAR GENETICIST (ON DNA IN AMBER)

Nature as a whole possesses a store of force which cannot in any way be either increased or diminished.

HERMANN VON HELMHOLTZ (1821–1894)
GERMAN PHYSIOLOGIST

The wood does not live as we live, restless and running, panting after flesh, and even in sleep tossing with fears. It is aloof from thoughts and instincts; it responds, but only to the sun and wind, the rock and the stream — never, though you shout yourself hoarse, to propaganda, temptation, reproach, or promises. You cannot . . . preach to a tree how it shall attain the kingdom of heaven. It is already closer to it, up there, than you will grow to be. . . . If you burn it, cut, hack through it with a blade, it angrily repairs the green leaves again, toiling, adjusting breathing — forgetting you.

DONALD CULROSS PEATTIE (1898–1964)
U.S. BIOLOGIST-NATURALIST

An organism has a sort of fluid form like that of a waterfall, through which water ceaselessly is pouring but which keeps in its descent a definite pattern.

EDMUND W. SINNOTT (1888–1968)
U.S. BIOLOGIST

Sexuality is the one aspect of biological being in which, unbeknownst to ourselves, we are in the grip of a power serving ends beyond ourselves. This is true of the animal kingdom generally speaking. One sees it most dramatically in the notorious case of salmon, who go upstream to spawn, but at the cost of their own lives.

LEON R. KASS (B. 1939), U.S. BIOLOGIST

When a race of plants is once pretty well established, the seedraisers do not pick out the best plants, but merely go over their seed-beds, and pull up the "rogues," as they call the plants that deviate from the proper standard. With animals this kind of selection is, in fact, likewise followed; for hardly any one is so careless as to breed from his worst animals.

CHARLES DARWIN (1809–1882)
BRITISH BIOLOGIST

Spiders always weave their webs in three dimensions, and when a spider finds that there is insufficient space to attach certain threads in the third dimension, it leaves the place and seeks another, instead of finishing the web in a single plane. . . . For a spider to change the pattern of its web is as impossible as for an inexperienced man to build a bridge across a chasm obstructing his way.

ALEXANDER PETRUNKEVITCH (1875–1964)
RUSSIAN ZOOLOGIST

Most scientists and philosophers now agree that nothing is truly random in the natural world.

DAVID M. RAUP (B. 1933), U.S. PALEONTOLOGIST

Life, so to speak, imposes organization upon matter. . . . Evidently each tiny living unit is a much more complex thing than it appears to be for it bears within itself an image of the whole organism, the "goal" toward which its development persistently will move.

EDMUND W. SINNOTT (1888–1968)
U.S. BIOLOGIST

In front of each natural entity there stands "a picture of what it ought to be," a form for whose realization it strives with all its powers.

KARL HEIM (1874–1958)
GERMAN RESEARCH SCIENTIST

FACES OF CHANGE

Life as a whole is a ceaseless change. . . . There is no sign of a physical limit yet.

HERMANN JOSEPH MULLER (1890–1967)
U.S. SCIENTIST

Flowers changed the face of the planet. Without them, the world we know — even man himself would never have existed. Francis Thompson, the

English poet, once wrote that one could not pluck a flower without troubling a star. Intuitively he had sensed like a naturalist the enormous interlinked complexity of life. . . . The weight of a petal has changed the face of the world and made it ours.

LOREN EISELEY (1907–1977)
U.S. ANTHROPOLOGIST

Nature proceeds little by little from things lifeless to animal life in such a way that it is impossible to determine the exact line of demarcation, nor on which side thereof an intermediate form should lie.

ARISTOTLE (384–322 B.C.)
GREEK PHILOSOPHER-SCIENTIST

It might be a great advantage to the hive-bee to have a slightly longer or differently constructed proboscis. . . . It might be a great advantage to the red clover to have a shorter or more deeply divided tube to its corolla, so that the hive-bee could visit its flowers. Thus I can understand how a flower and a bee might slowly become, either simultaneously or one after the other, modified and adapted in the most perfect manner to each other. . . .

CHARLES DARWIN (1809–1882)
BRITISH BIOLOGIST

The periods of rapid change tend to be lost between the cracks of the paleontologist's time scale.

JEFFREY S. LEVINTON (B. 1946)
U.S. EVOLUTIONARY BIOLOGIST

I'm convinced a meteorite ripped into the earth. It certainly, I think, killed off my beautiful ammonites.

PETER A. WARD (B. 1934), U.S. PALEONTOLOGIST

The one universal ever-operating law throughout has been the law of change. Nature never stands still and never duplicates herself. Life is always in the process of becoming something else.

LAURENCE M. GOULD (B. 1896), U.S. SCIENTIST

Nature does not proceed by leaps.

CAROLUS LINNAEUS (1707–1778)
SWEDISH BOTANIST

NOT SO NATURAL

All things are artificial, for nature is the art of God.

SIR THOMAS BROWNE (1605–1682)
BRITISH MEDICAL RESEARCHER

Since the measuring device has been constructed by the observer . . . we have to remember that what we observe is not nature in itself but nature exposed to our method of questioning.

WERNER KARL HEISENBERG (1901–1976)
GERMAN PHYSICIST

No man ever looks at the world with pristine eyes. He sees it edited by a definite set of customs and institutions and ways of thinking.

RUTH BENEDICT (1887–1948)
U.S. ANTHROPOLOGIST

The "control of nature" is a phrase conceived in arrogance, born of the Neanderthal age of biology and the convenience of man.

RACHEL CARSON (1907–1964)
U.S. MARINE BIOLOGIST

To me, fossils are sacred objects that should not be bought and sold. So when I came on one of my sites and saw that the fossils had just been chopped out of the wall with the intent of selling them to who knows . . . well, I just wanted to weep.

MICHAEL VOORHIES (B. 1941)
U.S. PALEONTOLOGIST

In the higher animals, at least, the signal that the balance is upset, the norm diverted, is not mere cessation of pleasure. It is pain. . . . It seems probable that some unease, some vague prototype of pain, some "tension," must be common to the whole organic world.

EDMUND W. SINNOTT (1888–1968)
U.S. BIOLOGIST

Well-washed and well-combed domestic pets grow dull; they miss the stimulus of fleas.

FRANCIS GALTON (1822–1911)
BRITISH SCIENTIST

This is the place where the hens lay colored eggs, where the tomatoes sprout whiskers, and the apples defy the law of gravity. Here magicians grow a hog that won't sunburn or a chicken with superdrumsticks or a bee with a better disposition. . . . They wake up the chrysanthemums at midnight for a stretch. . . . This is the Wonderland of Agriculture where scientists build birds, beasts, bugs to order. It is the United States Department of Agriculture's Research center . . . where new types of plants and animals are turned out to blueprint specifications, just like new-model automobiles. . . .

ALFRED TOOMBS (B. 1912)
U.S. SCIENTIST

The savannah's going bananas.

PETER WARSHALL, U.S. ARID PLANT SPECIALIST
(BIOSPHERE 2, ARIZONA, 1991–1993)

Everything in excess is opposed to nature.

HIPPOCRATES (460–400 B.C.)
GREEK, "FATHER OF MEDICINE"

THE SPIRIT OF NATURE

You can throw yourself flat on the ground, stretched
out upon Mother Earth, with the certain conviction
that you are one with her and she with you. . . . As
surely as she will engulf you tomorrow, so surely
will she bring you forth anew.

ERWIN SCHRÖDINGER (1887–1961)
AUSTRIAN PHYSICIST

Nature herself is wild and rich and her splendor is
unconstrained.

MICHAEL J. KATZ (B. 1928), U.S. BIOLOGIST

An hour or two before the cold front arrives the
clouds in the sky become confused, somewhat like a
herd of cattle that smells the coyotes; but you observe that by intuition rather than by measurable
signs.

WOLFGANG LANGEWIESCHE (B. 1907)
GERMAN METEOROLOGIST

The scientist does not study nature because it is useful. . . . He studies it because he delights in it, and he

delights in it because it is beautiful.

JULES HENRI POINCARÉ (1854–1912)
FRENCH SCIENTIST

In my diary I find these quotations: "Science, art, literature, religion (except Christianity) originate in love of nature. Nature is the backbone of all education. Love is the great principle of nature and life."

MARGARET MORSE NICE (1883–1974)
U.S. ORNITHOLOGIST

The world, the natural world, looks very good to me, and tastes good and smells good and has a very good feel in all its textures of bark and blossom and feathers and fur and plain dark dirt. . . . There come back to me across the years the words of an old naturalist . . . talking about his love for watching birds and animals: "They are our childhood come back to us, all instinct and joy and adventure." That is just about it, I think.

ALAN DEVOE (1909–1955), U.S. NATURALIST

Look! The silk in the milkweed pods is what the fairies use to stuff their mattresses. Blow on the dandelion down to make a wish. . . . Pause in the middle of fantasy to see the natural world as fragile and precious, threatened as well as caressed by human dreaming.

MARY CATHERINE BATESON (B. 1939)
U.S. ANTHROPOLOGIST

Nature need not adhere to human standards, and she need not follow human principles.

MICHAEL J. KATZ (B. 1928), U.S. BIOLOGIST

The equations we seek are the poetry of nature. . . .

Why is nature that way? Why is it possible for these powerful manifestations of forces to be trapped in a very simple, beautiful formula? This has been a question which many people have discussed, but there's no answer.

CHEN NING YANG (B. 1922), U.S. PHYSICIST

An obscure moth from Latin America saved Australia's pastureland from overgrowth by cactus ... the rosy periwinkle provided the cure for Hodgkin's disease and childhood lymphocytic leukemia ... the bark of the Pacific yew offers hope for victims of ovarian and breast cancer ... a chemical from the saliva of leeches dissolves blood clots during surgery. ...

EDWARD O. WILSON (B. 1929), U.S. BIOLOGIST

If we knew what makes a pine grow from a pine seed, and stay precisely a pine through all the vicissitudes of its history, we should come close to knowing what life really is.

EDMUND W. SINNOTT (1888–1968)
U.S. BIOLOGIST

Science shows us that the visible world is neither matter nor spirit; the visible world is the invisible organization of energy.

HEINZ R. PAGELS (B. 1939), U.S. PHYSICIST

My childhood was a very simple one. I grew up on a farm in Wisconsin. ... In those quiet moments in the woods I entered into an expanded state of consciousness in which I was able to perceive things beyond the normal human ranges of experience. I remember knowing where each small animal was without looking. I could sense its state. . . . Everything, including me, was living in a sea of energy.

BARBARA ANN BRENNAN [B. 1939]
U.S. PHYSICIST

The world of psychical phenomena appears to me to be as much a part of "Nature" as the world of physical phenomena; and I am unable to perceive any justification for cutting the Universe into two halves, one natural and one supernatural.

THOMAS H. HUXLEY (1825–1895)
BRITISH BIOLOGIST

Whatever its nature, beauty is the treasure that we value — a pattern of qualities in harmony with our spirits, something that vibrates on the same wave length as the living stuff of which we are composed.

EDMUND W. SINNOTT (1888–1968)
U.S. BIOLOGIST

The study of Nature is intercourse with the highest Mind. You should never trifle with Nature.

J. LOUIS R. AGASSIZ (1807–1873)
SWISS-AMERICAN ZOOLOGIST

VIEWS AND PERSPECTIVES

To a person uninstructed in natural history, his country or seaside stroll is a walk through a gallery filled with wonderful works of art, nine-tenths of which have their faces turned to the wall.

THOMAS H. HUXLEY (1825–1895)
BRITISH BIOLOGIST

Once a photograph of the Earth, taken from the outside, is available — once the sheer isolation of the
Earth becomes plain — a new idea as powerful as
any in history will be let loose.

SIR FRED HOYLE (B. 1915)
BRITISH ASTROPHYSICIST

Viewed from the distance of the moon, the astonish-
ing thing about the earth . . . is that it is alive. . . .
Aloft, floating free beneath the moist, gleaming
membrane of bright blue sky, is the rising earth, the
only exuberant thing in this part of the cosmos. . . .
It has the organized, self-contained look of a live
creature, full of information, marvelously skilled in
handling the sun.

LEWIS THOMAS (1913–1993), U.S. BIOLOGIST

If a microbe, living in one of the cracks of an elephant's skin, possessed our intelligence, and if his
ancestors had built up and transmitted to him a science, as ours have done in less than ten generations,
it is conceivable that he would not have a very clear
idea of the laws governing his universe: the elephant. The microbe lives at the bottom of a valley
one fifth of an inch deep, the equivalent to us of a
canyon six or seven thousand feet high. There he
may have created an image of his world very different from ours, and when the elephant scratches himself, or takes a bath, the microscopic dweller of the
valley can be excused if he attributes these unpre-
dictable cataclysms to an entirely different cause. Let
us try to avoid the point of view of the microbe, for

whom one day of twenty-four hours corresponds to a century, or four generations.

LECOMTE DU NOUY (1849–1919)
FRENCH SCIENTIST

What is the earth most like? . . . It is most like a single cell.

LEWIS THOMAS (1913–1993), U.S. BIOLOGIST

6

The World of the Scientist

QUEST OF DISCOVERY

I do not know what I may appear to the world, but to myself I seem to have been only like a boy playing on the sea-shore, and diverting myself in now and then finding a smoother pebble and a prettier shell than ordinary, whilst the great ocean of truth lay all undiscovered before me.

SIR ISAAC NEWTON (1642–1727)
BRITISH PHYSICIST

We are more easily persuaded, in general, by the reasons we ourselves discover than by those which are given to us by others.

BLAISE PASCAL (1623–1662), FRENCH PHYSICIST

Come here! Hurry! There are little animals in this rain water.... Look! See what I have discovered!

ANTONIE VAN LEEUWENHOEK (1632–1723)
DUTCH MICROBIOLOGIST

The butterflies are fluttering, but you feed off fear as if it's a high-energy candy bar. It keeps you alert and focused ... you know you can be hammered by something unexpected, but you count on your experience, concentration, and instincts to pull you through. And luck.

CHARLES ELWOOD YEAGER (B. 1923)
U.S. RESEARCH PILOT

Any scientist who is not a hypocrite will admit the important part that luck plays in scientific discovery.

SIR PETER BRIAN MEDAWAR (1915–1987)
BRITISH ZOOLOGIST

I didn't explode with excitement. I was in a rock shop where they sell things. I didn't want to seem overly excited because I didn't want the owner to think she had something that was worth millions of dollars. I looked at it, and I turned to Bob and I said, "You're not going to believe this, but this is a baby hadrosaur." And Bob said, "Bull——."

JACK HORNER (B. 1946), U. S. PALEONTOLOGIST

This is going to make me a famous guy, if it works.

KARY MULLIS (B. 1944), U. S. BIOCHEMIST
(WON THE NOBEL PRIZE, 1993, FOR COPYING DNA)

Don't laugh ... I felt I was born for that moment. To stand there, on that street in Paris in the middle of the night, with this idea at last clarified in my mind. Oh, that clarification! It was as though the idea had come into my head so that one day I would know the incredible joy of that clarification. Nothing else can touch that experience for me. Let me tell you, there's not an "I love you" in the world that can touch it. Nothing.

LAURA LEVIN, U.S. BIOPHYSICIST
(DISCOVERING THE MUSCLE MECHANISM OF THE CLAM)

It is like finding the handwriting of God.

JOE PRIMACK (B. 1945), U.S. ASTROPHYSICIST
(ON DISCOVERING "RIPPLES" IN SPACE)

The joy of insight is a sense of involvement and awe, the elated state of mind that you achieve when you have grasped some essential point; it is akin to what you feel on top of a mountain after a hard climb or when you hear a great work of music.

VICTOR WEISSKOPF (B. 1908)
AUSTRIAN-AMERICAN PHYSICIST

I have gazed on the face of Agamemnon.

HEINRICH SCHLIEMANN (1822–1890)
GERMAN ARCHEOLOGIST

I don't know what that something is yet. But I can taste it.

STUART A. KAUFFMAN (B. 1939)
U.S. THEORETICAL BIOLOGIST

Suddenly, as I was walking down a London street, I asked myself: "Relative to *what*?" The solid ground failed beneath my feet. With the familiar leaping of the heart I had my first sense of the Cosmos. When I tried to tell Miss Pendlebury of the experience, she remarked calmly that I should find Relativity very interesting. . . . There is nothing personal in the thunderclap of understanding. The lightning that releases it comes from outside oneself.

CECILIA PAYNE GAPOSCHKIN (1900–1979)
BRITISH ASTRONOMER

The knocking down of the six men was performed with two of my large jars not fully charged. . . . I applied the other end of my rod to the prime-conductor, and they all dropped together. . . . Too great a charge might, indeed, kill a man, but I have not yet seen any hurt done by it. It would certainly, as you observe, be the easiest of all deaths. . . .

BENJAMIN FRANKLIN (1706–1790)
U.S. SCIENTIST

I love fools' experiments; I am always making them.

CHARLES DARWIN (1809–1882)
BRITISH BIOLOGIST

Besides learning to see, there is another art to be learned — not to see what is not.

MARIA MITCHELL (1818–1889)
U.S. ASTRONOMER

In completing one discovery we never fail to get an imperfect knowledge of others of which we could have no idea before, so that we cannot solve one doubt without creating several new ones.

JOSEPH PRIESTLEY (1733–1804)
BRITISH CHEMIST

We did not know at the beginning how to put the uranium or the plutonium together fast enough to avoid the explosion starting at a stage where it would not yield sufficient power. . . . The psychological reactions to these difficulties were varied. Some of us, including myself, secretly wished that the difficulties would be insurmountable. We were all aware that the bomb we were trying to develop would be such a terrible means of destruction that the world might be better off without it. And if it was impossible for anyone to develop a nuclear bomb, there wouldn't be any danger of the Nazis having one.

VICTOR WEISSKOPF (B. 1908)
AUSTRIAN-AMERICAN PHYSICIST

In ancient days two aviators procured to themselves
wings. Daedalus flew safely through the middle air
and was duly honored on his landing. Icarus soared
upwards to the sun till the wax melted which bound
his wings and his flight ended in fiasco.... Cautious
Daedalus will apply his theories where he feels confi-
dent they will safely go; but by his excesses of caution their hidden weaknesses remain undiscovered.
Icarus will strain his theories to the breaking point
till the weak points gape.

SIR ARTHUR EDDINGTON (1882–1944)
BRITISH THEORETICAL ASTRONOMER

Results! Why, man, I have gotten a lot of results. I
know several thousand things that won't work.

THOMAS ALVA EDISON (1847–1931)
U.S. SCIENTIST

I feel that the greatest reward for doing is the opportunity to do more.

JONAS SALK (B. 1914), U.S. MICROBIOLOGIST

If I have ever made any valuable discoveries, it has
been owing more to patient attention, than to any
other talent.

SIR ISAAC NEWTON (1642–1727)
BRITISH PHYSICIST

One day we were sitting in a coffeehouse outside a
sports building with a swimming pool, discussing
this problem, when [Werner K.] Heisenberg said,
"Look at how people go in and come out of that
building all dressed. Do you conclude that they were
dressed in the pool?" As it turned out, the electron
does not come from inside the nucleus but is created

near the nucleus.

VICTOR WEISSKOPF (B. 1908)
AUSTRIAN-AMERICAN PHYSICIST

The problem when solved will be simple.

CHARLES FRANKLIN KETTERING (1876–1958)
U.S. INVENTOR

No, it's a great life. It's harder than I ever imagined, in the sense that you have to get used to wasting an enormous amount of time. You have to get the discipline of sitting at your desk fooling around with ideas that almost never work and living for the rare moment when an idea does work.

STEVEN WEINBERG (B. 1933), U.S. PHYSICIST

Give me where to stand, and I will move the earth.

ARCHIMEDES (287–212 B.C.), GREEK INVENTOR

HERE TODAY, GONE TOMORROW

On any Tuesday morning, if asked, a good working scientist will tell you with some self-satisfaction that the affairs of his field are nicely in order, that things are finally looking clear and making sense, and all is well. But come back again on another Tuesday, and the roof may have just fallen in on his life's work.

LEWIS THOMAS (1913–1993), U.S. BIOLOGIST

I have steadily endeavored to keep my mind free so as to give up any hypothesis, however much beloved (and I cannot resist forming one on every subject), as soon as the facts are shown to be opposed to it.

CHARLES DARWIN (1809–1882)
BRITISH BIOLOGIST

A null result would kill off the whole present crop of theories.

PHILIP LUBIN (B. 1953)
U.S. ASTROPHYSICIST

No amount of experimentation can ever prove me right; a single experiment may at any time prove me wrong.

ALBERT EINSTEIN (1879–1955)
SWISS-AMERICAN PHYSICIST

7

The Mind

BOUNTIFUL KNOWLEDGE

Whatever a man does he must do first in his mind.

ALBERT SZENT-GYÖRGYI (1893–1986)
HUNGARIAN-AMERICAN BIOCHEMIST

If one consciously fills his mind with a goal, the time will soon arrive when deliberate effort of attention is no longer necessary, for the compass-needle of his heart swings naturally toward its new pole.

EDMUND W. SINNOTT (1888–1968)
U.S. BIOLOGIST

We are an intelligent species and the use of our intelligence quite properly gives us pleasure. In this respect the brain is like a muscle. When it is in use we feel very good. Understanding is joyous.

CARL SAGAN (B. 1934), U.S. ASTRONOMER

Mind is the highest of biological phenomena, but it is a biological process, nevertheless.

EDMUND W. SINNOTT (1888–1968)
U.S. BIOLOGIST

We have maybe ten billion neurons. Each neuron has something like 10,000 to 100,000 synapses or connections. So this is a very complicated thing — but nevertheless, it's finite. . . . Therefore, there will be a final limit to the human ability to comprehend the most subtle, the most beautiful, the most complex questions.

CHEN NING YANG (B. 1922), U.S. PHYSICIST

Intelligence . . . does not seem to have increased rapidly in depth during the last 10,000 years. As much intelligence was needed to invent the bow and arrow, when starting from nothing, as to invent the machine gun, with the help of all the anterior inventions. Confucius, Lao Tse, Buddha, Democritus, Pythagoras, Archimedes, Plato were as intelligent as Bacon, Descartes, Pascal, Newton, Kepler, Bergson, and Einstein. But why should intelligence increase? It was prodigious in former times, and is just as astounding today. . . . There seems no more reason for it to increase than for a bird's wing or an eye to perfect itself.

LECOMTE DU NOUY (1849–1919)
FRENCH SCIENTIST

If a little knowledge is dangerous, where is the man who has so much as to be out of danger?

THOMAS H. HUXLEY (1825–1895)
BRITISH BIOLOGIST

Our intellectual endeavors, our whole science will be of no avail if they do not lead man to a better comprehension of himself, of the meaning of his life, and of the resources buried in his inner self.

LECOMTE DU NOUY (1849–1919)
FRENCH SCIENTIST

To doubt everything or to believe everything are two equally convenient solutions; both dispense with the necessity of reflection.

JULES HENRI POINCARÉ (1854–1912)
FRENCH SCIENTIST

Nothing in life is to be feared. It is only to be understood.

MARIE CURIE (1867–1934), POLISH CHEMIST

Half the physical misery of life could be cured by a little knowledge and restraint.

SIR J. ARTHUR THOMSON (1861–1933)
SCOTTISH BIOLOGIST

All of us have known men and women of very modest natural gifts and with intelligence quotients no more than respectable, whose ambition and enthusiastic purposefulness were so strong as to carry their possessors on to high achievement.

EDMUND W. SINNOTT (1888–1968)
U.S. BIOLOGIST

Knowledge is experience. Anything else is just information.

ALBERT EINSTEIN (1879–1955)
SWISS-AMERICAN PHYSICIST

If you know what you know, and know what you don't know, that is true knowledge.

CHEN NING YANG (B. 1922), U.S. PHYSICIST
(QUOTING AN ANCIENT CHINESE SAYING)

THE LEARNED

We know too much for one man to know much.

J. ROBERT OPPENHEIMER (1904–1967)
U.S. PHYSICIST

We don't know a millionth of one percent about anything.
                          THOMAS ALVA EDISON (1847–1931)
                                           U.S. SCIENTIST

We have brains — and minds — because our hungry
ancestors had to evolve them to keep from starving.
                          EDMUND W. SINNOTT (1888–1968)
                                           U.S. BIOLOGIST

Man is the only animal that knows nothing, and can
learn nothing without being taught. He can neither
speak nor walk nor eat, nor do anything at the
prompting of nature, but only weep.
        PLINY THE ELDER (23–70 A.D.), ROMAN NATURALIST

You cannot teach a man anything; you can only help
him find it within himself.
                          GALILEO GALILEI (1564–1642)
                          ITALIAN PHYSICIST-ASTRONOMER

Man is inside his most important biological speci-
men, *himself*, and . . . from this strategic position he
is able to learn many things that no amount of observation of other specimens ever could reveal.
                          EDMUND W. SINNOTT (1888–1968)
                                           U.S. BIOLOGIST

A man has always to be busy with his thoughts if
anything is to be accomplished.
               ANTONIE VAN LEEUWENHOEK (1632–1723)
                                 DUTCH MICROBIOLOGIST

In a free world, if it is to remain free, we must maintain, with our lives if need be, but surely by our
lives, the opportunity for a man to learn anything.
                          J. ROBERT OPPENHEIMER (1904–1967)
                                           U.S. PHYSICIST

The most extraordinary thing about a really good
teacher is that he or she transcends accepted educa-
tional methods. Such methods are designed to help
average teachers approximate the performance of
good teachers.

MARGARET MEAD (1901–1978)
U.S. ANTHROPOLOGIST

If one cannot state a matter clearly enough so that
even an intelligent twelve-year-old can understand
it, one should remain within the cloistered walls of
the university and laboratory until one gets a better
grasp of one's subject matter.

MARGARET MEAD (1901–1978)
U.S. ANTHROPOLOGIST

My advice to young working men desirous of better-
ing their circumstances, and adding to the amount of
their enjoyment, is a very simple one. Do not seek
happiness in what is misnamed pleasure; seek it
rather in what is termed study. Keep your con-
sciences clear, your curiosity fresh, and embrace
every opportunity of cultivating your minds. . . .

HUGH MILLER (1802–1856)
SCOTTISH GEOLOGIST

The only medicine for suffering, crime, and all other
woes of mankind, is wisdom. Teach a man to read
and write, and you have put into his hands the great
keys of the wisdom box. But it is quite another thing
to open the box. . . . Perhaps the most valuable result
of all education is the ability to make yourself do the
thing you have to do, when it ought to be done,
whether you like it or not; it is the first lesson that
ought to be learned; and however early a man's

training begins, it is probably the last lesson that he learns thoroughly.

THOMAS H. HUXLEY (1825–1895)
BRITISH BIOLOGIST

THE SCIENTIFIC BENT

Facts compel me to conclude that my brain was never formed for much thinking.

CHARLES DARWIN (1809–1882)
BRITISH BIOLOGIST

Excessive intelligence, which creates an Archimedes or a Descartes, anesthetizes the more subtle qualities of the brain. . . .

LECOMTE DU NOUY (1849–1919)
FRENCH SCIENTIST

Those who are not shocked when they first come across quantum theory cannot possibly have understood it.

NIELS BOHR (1885–1962), DANISH PHYSICIST

The whole of science is nothing more than a refinement of everyday thinking.

ALBERT EINSTEIN (1879–1955)
SWISS-AMERICAN PHYSICIST

In the fields of observation, chance favors only the mind that is prepared.

LOUIS PASTEUR (1822–1895)
FRENCH CHEMIST-MICROBIOLOGIST

To function as a citizen, you need to know a little bit about a lot of different sciences — a little biology, a little geology, a little physics, and so on. . . . The scientifically illiterate person has been cut off from an enriching part of life, just as surely as a person who cannot read.

ROBERT M. HAZEN (B. 1948)
U.S. GEOPHYSICAL SCIENTIST

Learn the ABC of science before you try to ascend its summit.

IVAN PETROVICH PAVLOV (1849–1936)
RUSSIAN PHYSIOLOGIST

BEYOND REASON

There is no logical way to the discovery of . . . elemental laws. There is only the way of intuition, which is helped by a feeling for the order lying behind the appearance.

ALBERT EINSTEIN (1879–1955)
SWISS-AMERICAN PHYSICIST

Our current struggle may thus be only a foretaste of a completely new form of human intellectual endeavor, one that will not only lie outside physics but will not even be describable as "scientific."

G. F. CHEW (B. 1924), U.S. PHYSICIST

I suspect it is the involuntary faculty of thought that gives rise to what we call "a flash of intuition," something that I imagine must be merely the result of unnoticed thinking.

ISAAC ASIMOV (1920–1992), U.S. BIOCHEMIST

Because of this age-long training in human relations — for that is what feminine intuition really is — women have a special contribution to make to any group enterprise. . . .

MARGARET MEAD (1901–1978)
U.S. ANTHROPOLOGIST

Frequently I had to use my intuition. Intuition in science consists of half-conscious knowledge — a certain feeling of how things work even if no exact information is available. . . . My office was dubbed the seat of "the oracle," or less reverently, "the cave of hot air." I was constantly asked to predict neutron effect. Mostly I was right; sometimes nature knew better.

VICTOR WEISSKOPF (B. 1908)
AUSTRIAN-AMERICAN PHYSICIST

Mind is not something limited to the human brain, or to any brain, but its primitive beginnings are to be found in the activity of every living cell.

EDMUND W. SINNOTT (1888–1968)
U.S. BIOLOGIST

The stuff of thought is not caged in the brain but is scattered all over the body. . . .

RICHARD M. BERGLAND (B. 1932)
U.S. MEDICAL RESEARCHER

Your mind is in every cell of your body.

CANDACE PERT (B. 1946)
U.S. NEURO RESEARCHER

The human mind is not only enabled to number worlds beyond the unassisted ken of mortal eye, but to trace the events of indefinite ages before the creation of our race.

SIR CHARLES LYELL (1797–1875)
BRITISH GEOLOGIST

This man [a former anthropology teacher] was extraordinary. In his presence, or in reading his writings, I always had the feeling that his mind was off the scale. I knew him only at the end of his life, when he was a man of failing health and failing powers. One day I went to visit him in the hospital, as I'd done a number of times before. . . . I walked into the room, and there he was, lying in bed, very peaceful. Had I not been told by the nurse, I would have assumed he was asleep. I don't really know what happened in the next few moments, but I found myself on my knees at the end of the bed. I was thunderstruck. Here he was, but he wasn't there at all. There was almost a smile on his face. All I could think of was — where is he? Where is this mind? What's happened to it?

MARY CATHERINE BATESON (B. 1939)
U.S. ANTHROPOLOGIST

8

Truth

SCIENTIFIC TRUTHS

Science is the search for truth — it is not a game in which one tries to beat his opponent, to do harm to others.

LINUS PAULING (B. 1901), U.S. CHEMIST

Science is knowledge arranged and classified according to truth, facts, and the general laws of nature.

LUTHER BURBANK (1849–1926)
U.S. HORTICULTURAL SCIENTIST

Every great scientific truth goes through three stages. First, people say it conflicts with the Bible. Next they say it had been discovered before. Lastly, they say they always believed it.

J. LOUIS R. AGASSIZ (1807–1873)
SWISS-AMERICAN ZOOLOGIST

I say that as concerns the truth, of which mathematical demonstrations give us the knowledge, it is the same as that which the Divine Wisdom knows.

GALILEO GALILEI (1564–1642)
ITALIAN PHYSICIST-ASTRONOMER

The time has come when scientific truth must cease to be the property of the few, when it must be woven into the common life of the world.

J. LOUIS R. AGASSIZ (1807–1873)
SWISS-AMERICAN ZOOLOGIST

I cannot prove scientifically that truth must be conceived as a truth that is valid independent of humanity; but I believe it firmly.

ALBERT EINSTEIN (1879–1955)
SWISS-AMERICAN SCIENTIST

STICKS AND STONES

It is an old story. . . . Giordano Bruno, who fought for scientific knowledge and against astrological superstition, was condemned to death by the Inquisition. It is the same psychic pestilence which delivered Galileo to the Inquisition, let Copernicus die in misery, made Leeuwenhoek a recluse, drove Nietzsche into insanity, Pasteur and Freud into exile. It is the indecent, vile attitude of contemporaries of all times.

WILHELM REICH (1897–1957), U.S. SCIENTIST

Skepticism in this field is like weeds. It is a problem. And it comes from people who know very little or nothing and all of a sudden become experts. So it is pointless to overcome it, for skepticism will always be around, no matter what it is, whether it be on the paranormal or the psychic. There will always be skeptics.

AARON ABRAHAMSEN (B. 1921)
U.S. AERONAUTICAL SCIENTIST

Religion and natural science are fighting a joint battle
in an incessant, never relaxing crusade against skepticism and against dogmatism, against disbelief and
against superstition, and the rallying cry in this crusade has always been, and always will be, "On to
God."
MAX PLANCK (1858–1947)
GERMAN PHYSICIST

I have been publicly discussed, lambasted and lam-
pooned, lionized and mythologized, called an institu-
tion and a stormy petrel, and cartooned as a candidate
for Presidency, wearing a human skull around my
neck as an ornament. . . . Those whose lives I have
touched — and still touch — have to deal with all this
also.
MARGARET MEAD (1901–1978)
U.S. ANTHROPOLOGIST

Whereas you, Galileo, son of the late Vincenzio Galilei, of Florence, aged 70 years, were denounced in
1615, to this Holy Office, for holding as true a false
doctrine taught by many, namely, that the sun is im-
movable in the centre of the world . . . we pronounce
this Our final sentence. . . . We condemn you to the
formal prison of this Holy Office for a period deter-
minable at Our pleasure. . . .
GALILEO'S INQUISITION

I do not think you would wish anyone to conceal the
results at which he has arrived after he has worked
according to the best ability which may be in him. I
do not think my book will be mischievous; for there
are so many workers, that, if I be wrong, I shall soon
be annihilated; surely you will agree that truth can be

known only by rising victorious from every attack.

CHARLES DARWIN (1809–1882)
BRITISH BIOLOGIST

Should you destroy myself, as well as my house, library, and apparatus, ten more person, of equal or superior spirit and ability, would instantly rise up. If those ten were destroyed, an hundred would appear. . . . In this business we are the sheep and you the wolves.

JOSEPH PRIESTLEY (1733–1804)
BRITISH CHEMIST

If anyone doubts my veracity, I can only say that I pity his lack of faith.

RUDOLPH ERICH RASPE (1737–1794)
GERMAN MINERALOGIST

JUST THE FACTS

Facts are the air of science. Without them you never can fly.

IVAN PETROVICH PAVLOV (1849–1936)
RUSSIAN PHYSIOLOGIST

Philosophers and theologians have yet to learn that a physical fact is as sacred as a moral principle.

J. LOUIS R. AGASSIZ (1807–1873)
SWISS-AMERICAN ZOOLOGIST

It is as fatal as it is cowardly to blink facts because they are not to our taste.

JOHN TYNDALL (1820–1893), IRISH PHYSICIST

Sit down before fact like a child, and be prepared to give up every preconceived notion, follow humbly wherever and to whatever abysses Nature leads, or you shall learn nothing.

THOMAS H. HUXLEY (1825–1895)
BRITISH BIOLOGIST

Facts which at first seem improbable will, even on scant explanation, drop the cloak which has hidden them and stand forth in naked and simple beauty.

GALILEO GALILEI (1564–1642)
ITALIAN PHYSICIST-ASTRONOMER

Science is built up with facts, as a house is with stones. But a collection of facts is no more a science than a heap of stones is a house.

JULES HENRI POINCARÉ (1854–1912)
FRENCH SCIENTIST

In science, "fact" can only mean "confirmed to such a degree that it would be perverse to withhold provisional assent." I suppose the apples might start to rise tomorrow, but the possibility does not merit equal time in physics classrooms.

STEPHEN JAY GOULD (B. 1941)
U.S. GEOLOGIST-PALEONTOLOGIST

The plain fact is that there are no conclusions.

SIR JAMES JEANS (1877–1946)
BRITISH ASTRONOMER

It is the fate of theories to be washed away. . . . I hold them all very lightly, and have used them chiefly as convenient pegs on which to hang my collection of facts.

JAMES G. FRAZER (1854–1941)
BRITISH ANTHROPOLOGIST

Science is organized common sense where many a beautiful theory was killed by an ugly fact.

THOMAS H. HUXLEY (1825–1895)
BRITISH BIOLOGIST

Facts may seem like dry bones to the soaring imagination of the theorist. They are bones indeed, for they constitute the skeletal framework of the science, without which she could neither stand, nor walk, nor take the great leaps that have marked her progress in the last half century. . . .

CECILIA PAYNE GAPOSCHKIN (1900–1979)
BRITISH ASTRONOMER

TRUE AXIOMS

Ye shall know the truth, and the truth shall make you mad.

ALDOUS HUXLEY (1894–1964)
(GRANDSON, THOMAS HUXLEY, BRITISH BIOLOGIST)

Whoever undertakes to set himself up as a judge of Truth and Knowledge is shipwrecked by the laughter of the gods.

ALBERT EINSTEIN (1879–1955)
SWISS-AMERICAN PHYSICIST

I teach only the truth — but that shouldn't make you believe it.

MARTIN H. FISCHER (1879–1962)
U.S. SCIENTIST

Truth is the offspring of silent and unbroken meditation.

SIR ISAAC NEWTON (1642–1727)
BRITISH PHYSICIST

We know the truth, not only by the reason, but also by the heart.

BLAISE PASCAL (1623–1662), FRENCH PHYSICIST

What a blessing it would be if we could open and shut our ears as easily as we do our eyes.

GEORG CHRISTOPH LICHTENBERG (1742–1799)
GERMAN PHYSICIST

Time, whose tooth gnaws away at everything else, is powerless against the truth.

THOMAS H. HUXLEY (1825–1895)
BRITISH BIOLOGIST

Truth is what stands the test of experience. . . . The ideals which have lighted me on my way and time after time given me new courage to face life cheerfully, have been Truth, Goodness, and Beauty.

ALBERT EINSTEIN (1879–1955)
SWISS-AMERICAN PHYSICIST

Truth has no special time of its own. Its hour is now — always.

ALBERT SCHWEITZER (1875–1965)
ALSATIAN-BORN MEDICAL MISSIONARY

The high-minded man must care more for the truth than for what people think.

ARISTOTLE (384–322 B. C.)
GREEK PHILOSOPHER-SCIENTIST

9

Time

GREAT SPANS

In the morning of time the earth was a featureless ball of anarchic matter, hurtling down the dusty corridor of its orbit.

LINCOLN BARNETT (1909–1979)
U.S. SCIENCE WRITER

Globular clusters are believed to be among the first objects to form in our galaxy, and their age is estimated to be between thirteen and seventeen billion years. Obviously, the ages of the globular clusters cannot be older than the age of the universe itself.

WENDY L. FREEDMAN, U.S. ASTROPHYSICIST

Imagine the fifteen-billion-year lifetime of the universe compressed into the span of a single year. . . . Dinosaurs emerge on Christmas Eve; flowers arise on December 28TH; and men and women originate at 10:30 P.M. on New Year's Eve. All of recorded history occupies the last ten seconds of December 31. . . .

CARL SAGAN (B. 1934), U.S. ASTRONOMER

The created world is but a small parenthesis in eternity.

SIR THOMAS BROWNE (1605–1682)
BRITISH MEDICAL RESEARCHER

The elements life needs had to be cooked up in stars. The cooking time to get them was at least ten billion years.

JOHN BARROW (B. 1952), BRITISH PHYSICIST

I can prove the last fifteen billion years so I dictated it on my computer, which took almost as long as what I proved, which was only a brief moment in either case.

STEPHEN HAWKING (B. 1942)
BRITISH THEORETICAL PHYSICIST

Dinosaurs held sway for 100 million years while mammals, all the while, lived as small animals in the interstices of their world. After seventy million years on top, we mammals have an excellent track record and good prospects for the future, but we have yet to display the staying power of dinosaurs. People, on this criterion, are scarcely worth mentioning — five million years perhaps since Australopithecus, a mere 50,000 for our own species, Homo sapiens. Try the ultimate test within our system of values: Do you know anyone who would wager a substantial sum, even at favorable odds, on the proposition that Homo sapiens will last longer than Brontosaurus?

STEPHEN JAY GOULD (B. 1941)
U.S. GEOLOGIST-PALEONTOLOGIST

During the whole age of the reptiles, about 100 million years, the mammals vegetated. . . . The enormous dinosaurs, weighing up to eighty tons, could crush dozens of them underfoot without even being aware of it. Who could have foreseen in those days that the future belonged to these little beasts? . . .

LECOMTE DU NOUY (1849–1919)
FRENCH SCIENTIST

Looking out over the cove I felt a strong sense of the interchangeability of land and sea. . . . There was also an awareness of the past and of the continuing flow of time, obliterating much that had gone before, as the sea had that morning washed away the tracks of the bird. . . . There is a common thread that links these scenes and memories — the spectacle of life in all its varied manifestations as it has appeared, evolved, and sometimes died out.

RACHEL CARSON (1907–1964)
U.S. MARINE BIOLOGIST

WASTE NOT

A man who dares to waste one hour of life has not discovered the value of life.

CHARLES DARWIN (1809–1882)
BRITISH BIOLOGIST

The time is coming when every person who lays claim to ability will keep the question of waste before him constantly.   THOMAS ALVA EDISON (1847–1931)
U.S. SCIENTIST

Time is that wherein there is opportunity, and opportunity is that wherein there is no great time.

HIPPOCRATES (460–400 B.C.)
GREEK, "FATHER OF MEDICINE"

I cannot afford to waste my time making money.

J. LOUIS R. AGASSIZ (1807–1873)
SWISS-AMERICAN ZOOLOGIST

A MOMENT'S MEASURE

Life is a wave, which in no two consecutive moments of its existence is composed of the same particles.

JOHN TYNDALL (1820–1893), IRISH PHYSICIST

As no man fording a swift stream can dip his foot twice into the same water, so no man can, with exactness, affirm of anything in the sensible world that it is. As he utters the words, nay, as he thinks them, the predicate ceases to be applicable; the present has become the past; the "is" should be "was." And the more we learn of the nature of things, the more evident is it that what we call rest is only unperceived activity. . . .

THOMAS H. HUXLEY (1825–1895)
BRITISH BIOLOGIST

Usually, we pity the pet mouse or gerbil that lived its full span of a year or two at most. How brief its life, while we endure for the better part of a century. . . . I want to argue that such pity is misplaced. . . . Small mammals tick fast, burn rapidly, and live for a short time; large ones live long at a stately pace. Measured by their own internal clocks, mammals of different sizes tend to live for the same amount of time.

STEPHEN JAY GOULD (B. 1941)
U.S. GEOLOGIST-PALEONTOLOGIST

One of the difficulties in writing these recollections has been that the present is so much more interesting than the past. It is hard to keep one's attention on reminiscence.

MARGARET FLOY WASHBURN (1871–1939)
U.S. BEHAVIORAL SCIENTIST

10

War

POWERFUL ATOMS

We are living in the atomic age. It is a strange place for us to be. For none of us ever has seen an atom. Atoms are so minute that it would take the entire population of the earth 10,000 years to count the number of them in one drop of water. Before this count could be made, each of us would have to shrink to one-billionth of an inch in height to see what we were counting.

HOWARD W. BLAKESLEE (1880–1952)
U.S. SCIENTIST

We cannot control atomic energy to an extent which would be of any value commercially, and I believe we are not likely ever to be able to do so.

ERNEST RUTHERFORD (1871–1937)
BRITISH PHYSICIST

The power to destroy the world by the use of nuclear weapons is a power that cannot be used — we cannot accept the idea of such monstrous immorality.

LINUS PAULING (B. 1901), U.S. CHEMIST

Why was the second bomb dropped over Nagasaki?
The timing — just three days after Hiroshima — had
not permitted the Japanese government to sue for
peace had it wanted to. Could it have been that the
U.S. military was eager to see the effect of a plutonium bomb now that they knew what a uranium-235
bomb could accomplish, even though our test at
Alamogordo had shown that a plutonium bomb
would work as planned?

VICTOR WEISSKOPF (B. 1908)
AUSTRIAN-AMERICAN PHYSICIAN

Now we have met the villain. It consists of blobs of
penetrating energy produced by the popping off of
wound-up atoms. Some of these atoms nature herself winds up, but many of these the modern physicist has learned how to wind.

WARREN WEAVER (1894–1978), U.S. SCIENTIST

At the appointed time there was a blinding flash
lighting up the whole area brighter than the bright-
est daylight. A mountain range three miles from the
observation point stood out in bold relief. Then came
a tremendous sustained roar and a heavy pressure
wave which knocked down two men outside the control center. Immediately thereafter, a huge multi-col-
ored surging cloud boiled up to an altitude of over
40,000 feet. Clouds in its path disappeared. Soon the
shifting substratosphere winds dispersed the now
grey mass. The test was over, the project a success.

OFFICIAL STATEMENT, U.S. WAR DEPARTMENT

In some sort of crude sense which no vulgarity, no
humor, no overstatement can quite extinguish, the

physicists have known sin; and this is a knowledge which they cannot lose.

J. ROBERT OPPENHEIMER (1904–1967)
U.S. PHYSICIST
(TEST EXPLOSION OF THE ATOMIC BOMB,
LOS ALAMOS, NEW MEXICO, JULY 1945)

I saw [Werner K.] Heisenberg after the war, and he was completely changed from the man I had known. Before the war he had always struck me as an innocent Boy-Scout type, free of worries, youthful and enthusiastic. But when I saw him again, even his complexion had changed, and this was not due only to age. He visibly carried a load. I could not help thinking of Oscar Wilde's *The Picture of Dorian Gray* when I saw the imprint of those tragic years on his face.

VICTOR WEISSKOPF (B. 1908)
AUSTRIAN-AMERICAN PHYSICIST

I remember discussions with Bohr [in 1927] which went through many hours till very late at night and ended almost in despair; and when at the end of the discussion I went alone for a walk in the neighboring park I repeated to myself again and again the question: Can nature possibly be as absurd as it seemed to us in these atomic experiments?

WERNER KARL HEISENBERG (1901–1976)
GERMAN PHYSICIST

A massive discontinuity was introduced into life by the discovery of nuclear fission. We have to learn to live with it, for the alternative is that we do not live.

WARREN WEAVER (1894–1978), U.S. SCIENTIST

Science has brought forth this danger, but the real

problem is in the minds and hearts of men. . . . Peace cannot be kept by force.

ALBERT EINSTEIN (1879–1955)
SWISS-AMERICAN PHYSICIST

THE WARRIOR

When there is peace, science is constructive; when there is war, science is perverted to destructive ends.

RAYMOND B. FOSDICK (1883–1972)
U.S. SCIENTIST

I'm proud of the fact that I never invented weapons to kill.

THOMAS ALVA EDISON (1847–1931)
U.S. SCIENTIST

The man who enjoys marching in line and file to the strains of music falls below my contempt; he received his great brain by mistake — the spinal cord would have been amply sufficient. . . . To my mind, to kill in war is not a whit better than to commit ordinary murder.

ALBERT EINSTEIN (1879–1955)
SWISS-AMERICAN PHYSICIST

Can anything be more ridiculous than that a man has a right to kill men because he dwells on the other side of the water, and because his prince has a quarrel with mine, although I have none with him?

BLAISE PASCAL (1623–1662)
FRENCH PHYSICIST

Either man is obsolete or war is.

R. BUCKMINSTER FULLER (1895–1983)
U.S. INVENTOR

Man is not a blood-thirsty animal, and war is only due to the greed and lust for power of relatively small groups, the conspiracy of the few against the many.

ALBERT SZENT-GYÖRGYI (1893–1986)
HUNGARIAN-AMERICAN BIOCHEMIST

As for human nature, it contains no specific war instinct, as does the nature of harvester ants. There is in man's make-up a general aggressive tendency, but this, like all other human urges, is not a specific and unvarying instinct; it can be moulded into the most varied forms. It can be canalized into competitive sport, as in our own society, or as when certain Filipino tribes were induced to substitute football for head-hunting. It can be sublimated into non-competitive sport, like mountain-climbing, or into higher types of activity altogether, like exploration or research or social crusades.

JULIAN HUXLEY (1887–1975)
BRITISH ZOOLOGIST

Much can be done to change the nature of man himself. The intelligence which has converted the brother of the wolf into the faithful guardian of the flock ought to be able to do something toward curbing the instincts of savagery in civilized man.

THOMAS H. HUXLEY (1825–1895)
BRITISH BIOLOGIST

The next World War will be fought with stones.

ALBERT EINSTEIN (1879–1955)
SWISS-AMERICAN PHYSICIST

11

Progress

HUMAN HISTORY

Had Cleopatra's nose been shorter, the whole face of the world would have been different.

BLAISE PASCAL (1623–1662), FRENCH PHYSICIST

Human history has been molded by the aspirations of that minority of individuals who had the capacity to *want* something very much.

EDMUND W. SINNOTT (1888–1968)
U.S. BIOLOGIST

Science has done more for the development of western civilization in one hundred years than Christianity did in eighteen hundred years.

JOHN BURROUGHS (1837–1921), U.S. NATURALIST

The advance of science is not comparable to the changes of a city, where old edifices are pitilessly torn down to give place to new . . . but where an expert eye finds always traces of the prior work of the past centuries.

JULES HENRI POINCARÉ (1854–1912)
FRENCH SCIENTIST

In real life, every field of science is incomplete, and most of them — whatever the record of accomplishment during the last 200 years — are still in their very earliest stages.

LEWIS THOMAS (1913–1993), U.S. BIOLOGIST

The philosophies of one age have become the absurdities of the next, and the foolishness of yesterday has become the wisdom of tomorrow.

SIR WILLIAM OSLER (1849–1919)
CANADIAN RESEARCH SCIENTIST

The time will come when people will travel in stages moved by steam engines, from one city to another, almost as fast as birds fly, fifteen or twenty miles an hour.

OLIVER EVANS (1755–1819), U.S. INVENTOR

There are people who romanticize, who say, "Wouldn't it be nice to go back to the lovely old days when we didn't have pollution problems?" In a way it would — but we can't. . . . Those days weren't so terrific either. Many, many infants died within the first week of birth. Very few people lived the nice long lives that we're living now. Very few people could visit different parts of the globe. . . . We must advance new knowledge so that we have more ideas about how to deal with the continually new problems that we have.

MAXINE SINGER (B. 1931), U.S. GENETICIST

Reaching the Moon by three-man vessels in one long bound from Earth is like casting a thin thread across space. The main effort, in the coming decades, will be to strengthen this thread; to make it a cord, a cable, and, finally, a broad highway.

ISAAC ASIMOV (1920–1992), U.S. BIOCHEMIST

When it was suggested on April Fool's Day 1964 that
the proton consists of three quarks, no one suspected
that the quark concept was anything more than a
convenient mathematical way to organize the many
known elementary particles. . . . Quarks, however,
have since moved from mathematical fiction to physical reality in high-energy physics.

MARGARET L. SIBLER (EXPRESSED: 1985)
U.S. SCIENTIST

The world, which took but six days to make, is like to
take us six thousand years to make out.

SIR THOMAS BROWNE (1605–1682)
BRITISH RESEARCHER

REGRETS AND RESERVATIONS

The rapid progress true science now makes, occasions
my regretting sometimes that I was born so soon. . . .
O that moral science were in a fair way of improvement, that men would cease to be wolves to one another, and that human beings would at length learn
what they now improperly call humanity.

BENJAMIN FRANKLIN (1706–1790), U.S. SCIENTIST

By every conceivable measure, humanity is ecologi-
cally abnormal. Our species appropriates between
twenty and forty percent of the solar energy cap-
tured in organic material by land plants. There is no
way that we can draw upon the resources of the
planet to such a degree without drastically reducing
the state of most other species.

EDWARD O. WILSON (B. 1929), U.S. BIOLOGIST

If any society wishes to pay that cost for its chosen

and congenial traits, certain values will develop within this pattern, however "bad" it may be. But the risk is great, and the social order may not be able to pay the price. It may break down beneath them with all the consequent wanton waste of revolution and economic and emotional disaster.

RUTH BENEDICT (1887–1948)
U.S. ANTHROPOLOGIST

Civilized men arrived in the Pacific, armed with alcohol, syphilis, trousers, and the Bible.

HAVELOCK ELLIS (1859–1939), BRITISH SCIENTIST

As for the balance of nature, this is simply an arty phrase to denote the status quo, whatever exists in a certain place at a certain time. In truth, the status quo is always changing. On our Great Plains, for example, the balance of nature consisted for centuries of immense herds of bison browsing thunderously on buffalo grass. In the late 18th century the balance consisted of Indians, who acquired Spanish horses, slaughtering bison. Nowadays it consists of strip-farming, beauty shops, filling stations, beer cans. . . .

ROBERT WERNICK (B. 1928), U.S. ECOLOGIST

It is true that the laboratory and the X-ray have added much that is valuable to our knowledge of diagnosis, but in this change of tactics the average doctor has lost much of his basic skill. Thirty years ago, we had to depend upon our sense of touch, sight and hearing to make a diagnosis, and experience developed an alertness that is not completely replaced by routine laboratory reports. . . .

S. JOSEPHINE BAKER (1873–1945)
U.S. HEALTH RESEARCHER

Half the modern drugs could well be thrown out the window, except that the birds might eat them.

MARTIN H. FISCHER (1879–1962), U.S. SCIENTIST

As crude a weapon as the cave man's club, the chemical barrage has been hurled against the fabric of life.

RACHEL CARSON (1907–1964)
U.S. MARINE BIOLOGIST

We have been massively intervening in the environment. . . . Like the sorcerer's apprentice, we are acting upon dangerously incomplete knowledge. We are, in effect, conducting a huge experiment on ourselves.

BARRY COMMONER (B. 1917), U.S. BIOLOGIST

When I ask myself whether I would want to be a "test-tube person," I know that I would not like to have to add those self-doubts to my more ordinary repertory of insecurities.

RUTH HUBBARD (B. 1924), U.S. BIOLOGIST

Man's role is uncertain, undefined, and perhaps unnecessary.

MARGARET MEAD (1901–1978)
U.S. ANTHROPOLOGIST

There is no constructive solution to the world's problems except eventually a world government capable of establishing law over the entire surface of the earth.

HAROLD CLAYTON UREY (1893–1981)
U.S. SCIENTIST

Whether we look up at the sky or not, the question mark curls above our roofs and makes a mockery of our hopes. If your Earth is falling apart, there go your plans for summer vacation. . . .

JONATHAN WEINER (B. 1953), U.S. SCIENTIST

RESPONSIBILITY

Real human progress depends upon a good conscience.
ALBERT EINSTEIN (1879–1955)
SWISS-AMERICAN PHYSICIAN

Life is complicated, and getting more so, it seems, by the hour. One aspect of this — perhaps the central one of our times — is that science and technology have left the lab and the factory and are no longer the sole concern of scientists and engineers and their clients. Those fields of thought and action are now part of every one of our lives, no matter what our occupation, no matter where we live.
JAMES RUTHERFORD (B. 1925), U.S. SCIENTIST

If scientific research offers unimaginable opportunities for good, it imposes unexampled obligations to protect ourselves against equally unforeseeable dangers. . . . When man first discovered fire he began a long apprenticeship to caution in dealing with what is both useful and dangerous — and the end is not yet.
ALAN GREGG (EXPRESSED: 1949), U.S. BIOLOGIST

The scientist provides us with the knowledge and tools. He does not tell us how to use them. The solution rests with all of us.
HARLOW SHAPLEY (1885–1972), U.S. ASTRONOMER

Science can only ascertain what *is*, but not what *should be*, and outside of its domain value judgments of all kinds remain necessary.
ALBERT EINSTEIN (1879–1955)
SWISS-AMERICAN PHYSICIST

The future offers very little hope for those who expect that our new mechanical slaves will offer us a

world in which we may rest from thinking. Help us
they may, but at the cost of supreme demands upon
our honesty and our intelligence. The world of the
future will be an ever more demanding struggle
against the limitations of our intelligence, not a comfortable hammock in which we can lie down to be
waited upon by our robot slaves.

NORBERT WIENER (1894–1964), U.S. SCIENTIST

What does it matter if a large proportion of our population thinks that Chernobyl is a ski resort, DNA a
food additive, a megabyte an orthodontal problem,
and protons something you put on salad?

RICHARD P. BRENNAN, U.S. SCIENTIST

What difference does it make if some species are ex-
tinguished, if even half of all the species on Earth
disappear? Let me count the ways. . . . The loss of a
keystone species is like a drill accidentally striking a
power line. It causes lights to go out all over.

EDWARD O. WILSON (B. 1929), U.S. BIOLOGIST

Concern for man himself and his fate must always
form the chief interest of all technical endeavors . . .
in order that the creations of our mind shall be a
blessing and not a curse to mankind. Never forget
this in the midst of your diagrams and equations.

ALBERT EINSTEIN (1879–1955)
SWISS-AMERICAN PHYSICIST

Perhaps a time is coming when the nuclear arms race
of the past decades will be regarded as a serious case
of collective mental disease that was cured just in
time. If this happens, I will be able to have a clearer

conscience about my participation in developing the atomic bomb. Our original hope that the terrible destructive power of the bomb would make future world wars impossible may not have been in vain.

VICTOR WEISSKOPF (B. 1908)
AUSTRIAN-AMERICAN PHYSICIST

I date my own reawakening of interest in man's environment to the Apollo 8 mission and to the first clear photographs of the Earth from the missions. . . . Looking at the blackness beyond the sharp blue-green curve, trying to see even the place where the thin envelope of atmosphere and the solid Earth meet, the curious word "fragile" comes to mind. . . . I suspect that the greatest lasting benefit of the Apollo missions may be, if my hunch is correct, this sudden rush of inspiration to try to save this fragile environment. . . .

SIR FRED HOYLE (B. 1915)
BRITISH ASTROPHYSICIST

One needs to think not only about survival, but survival of what.

MARY CATHERINE BATESON (B. 1939)
U.S. ANTHROPOLOGIST

We face the future with a weapon in our hands that was not given to earlier rulers of the world — I mean scientific knowledge, and the capacity for increasing it indefinitely by scientific research.

SIR JAMES JEANS (1877–1946)
BRITISH ASTRONOMER

Science is another name for knowledge. . . . But knowledge is not enough. It must be tempered with justice, a sense of the moral life, and our capacity for love and community. Science brings us to a renewed appreciation of the human condition. . . .

HEINZ R. PAGELS (B. 1939), U.S. PHYSICIST

It is the devotion of oneself to an end which is far more important than the individual, the certainty that the end is absolutely good, not only for oneself but for all mankind, and the character to set personal advantage, comfort, and glory aside in the devoted effort to make even a little progress toward it.

OLIVER LA FARGE (1901–1963)
U.S. ANTHROPOLOGIST

Man's destiny is to be the sole agent for future evolution of this planet. . . . If he does not destroy himself, he has at least an equal stretch of evolutionary time before him to exercise his agency.

JULIAN HUXLEY (1887–1975)
BRITISH ZOOLOGIST

Advanced civilizations — if they exist — aren't breaking their backs to save us before we destroy ourselves. Personally, I think that makes for a more interesting universe.

CARL SAGAN (B. 1934), U.S. ASTRONOMER

If we hope to live a long time, we must begin to think like a geological force. That is, we must become the first geological force to learn to think.

J. B. S. HALDANE (1892–1964)
BRITISH GENETICIST

We men on earth are probably on a very low level, but we have our task like other and higher order of beings. As far as I can see — and I claim no prophetic insight — that task is to bring consciousness to the life of the earth — or, as Jung wrote in his old age, "to kindle a light in the darkness of mere being."

JOSEPH PRIESTLEY (1733–1804)
BRITISH CHEMIST

We must now transcend the Darwinian principle of natural selection and embrace a loftier standard that I call "the principle of cosmic selection."

ERIC J. CHAISSON (B. 1946)
U.S. ASTROPHYSICIST

FUTURE OF HOPE

My interest is in the future because I am going to spend the rest of my life there.

CHARLES FRANKLIN KETTERING (1876–1958)
U.S. INVENTOR

Nowhere has life's progress stopped, and nowhere can we see a limit to what it may achieve.

EDMUND W. SINNOTT (1888–1968)
U.S. BIOLOGIST

Yes, AIDS may run through the entire population, and may carry off a quarter or more of us. Yes, it may make no biological difference to Homo sapiens in the long run: there will still be plenty of us left and we can start again. Evolution cares as little for its agents — organisms struggling for reproductive success — as physics cares for individual atoms of hydrogen in the sun. But we care. These atoms are our neighbors, our lovers, our children and ourselves.

STEPHEN JAY GOULD (B. 1941)
U.S. GEOLOGIST-PALEONTOLOGIST

It is true that I deplore much in the present situation

in the world — basically due to overcrowding — yet for many of the features of civilization I am profoundly thankful: for instance, the comparative freedom of women, the advances in medical science, the availability of classical music on FM radio, the great improvements in photographic techniques, paperback books printed in America, electric refrigerators, electric and gas stoves, frozen foods . . . the convenience of the automobile, and the marvelous experience of flying over the earth. . . . We must try to open the eyes of the unseeing to the beauty and wonder of the earth. . . .

MARGARET MORSE NICE (1883–1974)
U.S. ORNITHOLOGIST

There are still a few of us left, though, who don't feel we're too good for the universe, no matter how much it lets us down. . . . Maybe it's more like a room after an all-night party, strewn with random debris by Someone whose idea of a good time we can never hope to fathom. I'd still like to know, still like to meet whoever's out there, still like to think my descendants won't be stuck here forever, toiling away on a large rock near a small-sized star. And for the time being, when I look up at night, I want to sense the huge, untidy humor of infinity — not a gravestone of our own making pressing down on us.

BARBARA EHRENREICH (B. 1941), U.S. BIOLOGIST

I never think of the future. It comes soon enough.

ALBERT EINSTEIN (1879–1955)
SWISS-AMERICAN PHYSICIST

Do not let yourselves be tainted by a deprecating and barren skepticism, do not let yourselves be discouraged by the sadness of certain hours which pass over nations. Live in the serene peace of laboratories and libraries. Say to yourselves first: What have I done for my instruction? and, as you gradually advance, What have I done for my country? until the time comes when you may have the immense happiness of thinking that you have contributed in some ways to the progress and good of humanity. . . .

LOUIS PASTEUR (1822–1895)
FRENCH CHEMIST-MICROBIOLOGIST

In recent times, modern science has developed to give mankind, for the first time in the history of the human race, a way of securing a more abundant life which does not simply consist in taking away from someone else.

KARL TAYLOR COMPTON (1887–1954)
U.S. PHYSICIST

The common attitude of men is forward-looking, purposeful.

EDMUND W. SINNOTT (1888–1968)
U.S. BIOLOGIST

12

The Human Condition

UNIQUE IDENTITY

Life is not easy for any of us. But what of that? We must have perseverance and above all confidence in ourselves. We must believe that we are gifted for something, and that this thing, at whatever cost, must be attained.

MARIE CURIE (1867–1934), POLISH CHEMIST

Man is a singular creature. He has a set of gifts which make him unique among the animals; so that, unlike them, he is not a figure in the landscape — he is a shaper of the landscape. In body and in mind he is the explorer of nature, the ubiquitous animal, who did not find but has made his home in every continent.

JACOB BRONOWSKI (1908–1974)
BRITISH SCIENTIST

Man does have motive power that is his own. He is not simply at the mercy of external agencies, strong and compelling as these obviously are. Something inside him helps direct his course. On the river of circumstance he still is borne along; but he moves there not inertly, like a log, but as a boat moves that contains within it power enough to give it steerage way at least, and sometimes even to carry it upstream against the current.

EDMUND W. SINNOTT (1888–1968)
U.S. BIOLOGIST

The man who regards his own life and that of his fellow creatures as meaningless is not merely unfortunate but almost disqualified for life.

ALBERT EINSTEIN (1879–1955)
SWISS-AMERICAN PHYSICIST

To say that human life is an accident on the stage of evolution, fundamentally no different from not only other animal life, but no different even from inorganic matter in motion, just doesn't square with the phenomena as we experience them.

MARY CATHERINE BATESON (B. 1939)
U.S. ANTHROPOLOGIST

I use the word "Humanist" to mean someone who believes that man is just as much a natural phenomenon as an animal or a plant. . . .

JULIAN HUXLEY (1887–1975)
BRITISH ZOOLOGIST

Human personality, tenuous as it may sometimes seem to be, is of surprisingly tough fiber. The knot of norms, goals, steady states, potencies, and purposes of which it is composed is almost impossible to loosen. To kill it is easy, and to direct the course of its development not difficult; but to break it down and make it into something different as a sculptor does with his clay; to shake it free from its past, to destroy its identity — this the organized pattern of personality most successfully resists.

EDMUND W. SINNOTT (1988–1968)
U.S. BIOLOGIST

The true value of a human being is determined by the measure and the sense in which he has attained liberation from the self.

ALBERT EINSTEIN (1879–1955)
SWISS-AMERICAN PHYSICIST

Science may someday provide us with a better understanding of ourselves, but never, I hope, with a set of technologies for doing something or other to improve ourselves. I am made nervous by assertions that human consciousness will someday be unraveled by research, laid out for close scrutiny like the workings of a computer. . . .

LEWIS THOMAS (1913–1993), U.S. BIOLOGIST

SOME BODY

We feel our toes from outside and from inside. We hear our heartbeats at night. We smell our sweat, we taste our blood. We are not all physicists or economists or mathematicians, but we are all biologists.

MICHAEL J. KATZ (B. 1928), U.S. BIOLOGIST

We speak of the body as a machine, but it is hardly necessary to say that none of the most ingenious machines set up by modern science can for a moment compare with it. The body is a self-building machine; a self-stoking, self-regulating, self-repairing machine — the most marvellous and unique automatic mechanism in the universe.

SIR J. ARTHUR THOMSON (1861–1933)
SCOTTISH BIOLOGIST

The "bookcase" in a cell is called the nucleus. The architect's plans run to forty-six volumes in man. . . . The "volumes" are called chromosomes. . . . The genes are strung out along them in order.

RICHARD DAWKINS (B. 1941)
BRITISH ZOOLOGIST

The best way to look at it is that a gene is like a sentence in an encyclopedia. It's a piece of information buried in the genome, the whole encyclopedia, which is a vast store of information. The gene instructs the cell how to do some one thing. All together, the trillions of cells in your body do all the things that make you who you are. . . .

MAXINE SINGER (B. 1931), U.S. GENETICIST

Genes and environment interact during development to produce something that is not reducible to "x" percent genes and "y" percent environment. . . . You bake the cake, and when you taste it you can't say five percent of the taste is due to the butter, ten percent is due to the flour, and so on. It is qualitatively different from the ingredients you started with.

STEVEN ROSE, (B. 1938)
U.S. BEHAVIOR GENETICIST

In some way the spinning electrons, the protons, and the score of other ultimate particles in matter are organized into atoms of carbon, hydrogen, oxygen, and nitrogen. These in turn combine to form huge molecules of protein. With various mineral elements

and an abundance of water they are built into protoplasm, and then, in some way quite unknown as yet,
this once dead matter suddenly comes to life. . . .
Here is born not only life but all that life can be.

EDMUND W. SINNOTT (1888–1968)
U.S. BIOLOGIST

We're special. And we are marvelous. There are many
living things in the world that are marvelous. How
does it diminish our sense of ourselves to understand
that we are the product of a lot of molecules coming
together in a marvelous way? We are not those molecules, we are all of them together.

MAXINE SINGER (B. 1931), U.S. GENETICIST

The body may be more than stuff, but the man
seems to be more than his body.

MARY CATHERINE BATESON (B. 1939)
U.S. ANTHROPOLOGIST

Man *is* a spirit, and it is as hard to fit him into a purely material mold as to weigh the beauty of a sym-
phony on a pair of scales. . . . The human spirit is a
glass through which we can peer more deeply into
reality than by purely rational instruments alone.

EDMUND W. SINNOTT (1888-1968)
U.S. BIOLOGIST

There is neither spirit nor matter in the world; the
"stuff of the universe" is spirit-matter. No other substance than this could produce the human molecule.

PIERRE TEILHARD DE CHARDIN (1881–1955)
JESUIT PALEONTOLOGIST

Modern science tells us that the human organism is
not just a physical structure made of molecules, but
that, like everything else, we are also composed of

energy fields. We are moving out of the world of static solid form into a world of dynamic energy fields. We, too, ebb and flow like the sea.

BARBARA ANN BRENNAN (B. 1939)
U.S. PHYSICIST

After all, our bodies are material systems and made of the same elements that form the substance of the earth and of the farthest stars.

EDMUND W. SINNOTT (1888–1968)
U.S. BIOLOGIST

Man is a microcosm, or a little world, because he is an extract from all the stars and planets of the whole firmament, from the earth and the elements; and so he is their quintessence.

THEOPHRASTUS PARACELSUS (1493–1541)
SWISS ALCHEMIST

Man's inescapable impasse is that he himself is part of the world he seeks to explore; his body and proudrain are mosaics of the same elemental particles that compose the dark, drifting dust clouds of interstellar space.

LINCOLN BARNETT (1909–1979)
SCIENCE WRITER

We literally are stardust.

JOHN L. HITCHCOCK (B. 1936), U.S. PHYSICIST

There is surely a piece of divinity in us, something that was before the elements, and owes no homage unto the sun.

SIR THOMAS BROWNE (1605–1682)
BRITISH MEDICAL RESEARCHER

Such, as far as one can tell it in so brief a space, is the tale of the wonderful mechanisms in the body. Even the skin, which binds and protects this marvellous system of parts, is a remarkable organ. . . . On the tender eyelids of a young child it is as thin as tissue paper, yet on the palms of some "horny-handed son of toil" it will produce protecting cells until it becomes an eighth of an inch thick. . . . "The proper study of mankind is man," said a great poet; and we may surely add that we know no more interesting study in the universe.

SIR J. ARTHUR THOMSON (1861–1933)
SCOTTISH BIOLOGIST

EMOTIONS

One of the most important facts about man is that he is a wanting, desiring, longing, aspiring animal. Indeed, this is the essence of him and the source of his power.

EDMUND W. SINNOTT (1888–1968)
U.S. BIOLOGIST

The natural man has only two primal passions, to get and to beget.

SIR WILLIAM OSLER (1849–1919)
CANADIAN RESEARCH SCIENTIST

My Dear Friend: I know of no Medicine fit to diminish the violent natural inclination you mention; and if I did, I think I should not communicate it to you. Marriage is the proper Remedy.

BENJAMIN FRANKLIN (1706–1790)
U.S. SCIENTIST

The forces that we see in nature, including the forces between the male and female, are chemical in origin, and the chemical forces are basically electric and magnetic forces, and we understand them very well.

CHEN NING YANG (B. 1922), U.S. PHYSICIST

Man puts himself at once on the level of the beast if he seeks to gratify lust alone, but he elevates his superior position when, by curbing the animal desire, he combines with the sexual functions ideas of morality, of the sublime, and of the beautiful.

BARON RICHARD VON KRAFFT-EBING (1840–1902)
GERMAN NEUROLOGIST

Man must have bread and butter, but he must also have something to lift his heart.

FAROUK EL BAZ (B. 1938), U.S. GEOLOGIST

Love alone is capable of uniting living beings in such a way as to complete and fulfill them, for it alone takes them and joins them by what is deepest in themselves.

PIERRE TEILHARD DE CHARDIN (1881–1955)
JESUIT PALEONTOLOGIST

The heart has its reasons, which reason does not know. We feel it in a thousand things.

BLAISE PASCAL (1623–1662), FRENCH PHYSICIST

Love is a conflict between reflexes and reflections.

MAGNUS HIRSCHFELD (1868–1935)
GERMAN SEXOLOGIST

Love is the climax of all goal-seeking, protoplasm's final consummation. To love your neighbor as yourself is the only basis for human relationships.

EDMUND W. SINNOTT (1888–1968)
U.S. BIOLOGIST

Anything will give up its secrets if you love it enough.

GEORGE WASHINGTON CARVER (1864–1943)
U.S. AGRICULTURAL SCIENTIST

Woman loves with her whole soul. To woman love is life, to man it is the joy of life.

BARON RICHARD VON KRAFFT-EBING (1840–1902)
GERMAN NEUROLOGIST

What makes us people and not computers is emotion.

EDWARD O. WILSON (B. 1929), U.S. BIOLOGIST

Many reformers think that emotions are a hindrance to man's attainment of the ideal society, and look forward to the day when reason only, unclouded by feeling, will guide his conduct. That day will never come, for emotion gives the motive power for behavior.

EDMUND W. SINNOTT (1888–1968), U.S. BIOLOGIST

Stones grow; Plants grow and live; Animals grow and live and feel.

CAROLUS LINNAEUS (1707–1778)
SWEDISH BOTANIST

Much of our failure to understand human nature arises from neglect of this need to have our faculties excited. . . . Excitement is not merely good; it is indispensable to a proper human life.

LANCELOT LAW WHYTE (1896–1972)
SCOTTISH PHYSICIST

In the beginning of my work, I matter-of-factly presumed that emotions were in the head or brain. Now I would say they are really in the body as well. They are expressed in the body and are part of the body. I can no longer make a strong distinction between the brain and the body.

CANDACE PERT (B. 1946)
U.S. NEURO-RESEARCHER

Dear reader or, better still, dear lady reader, recall the bright, joyful eyes with which your child beams upon you when you bring him a new toy, and then let the physicist tell you that in reality nothing emerges from these eyes: in reality their only objectively detectable function is, continually, to be hit by and to receive light quanta.

GERHARD STAGUHN (B. 1952), U.S. PHYSICIST

Laughter is man's most distinctive emotional expression. Man shares. Laughter is man's most distinctive emotional expression. Man shares the capacity for love and hate, anger and fear, loyalty and grief, with other living creatures. But humor, which has an intellectual as well as an emotional element, belongs to man.

MARGARET MEAD (1901–1978)
U.S. ANTHROPOLOGIST

There are some things that are so serious you can only joke about them.

NIELS BOHR (1885–1962), DANISH PHYSICIST

The lure of happiness and the fear of pain are fundamental qualities possessed by all living things and are the two forces which have through untold millenniums kept what we usually call life from destruction. . . .

LUTHER BURBANK (1849–1926)
U.S. HORTICULTURAL SCIENTIST

Without pain's warning we should run past the danger signals until it was too late to restore the threatened balance of life. Pain is therefore not mere meaningless suffering. There is a reason for it. It has importance for survival.

EDMUND W. SINNOTT (1888–1968)
U.S. BIOLOGIST

To penetrate into the heart of the thing — even a little thing, a blade of grass, as Walt Whitman said — is to experience a kind of exhilaration that, it may be, only human beings of all the beings on this planet can feel.

CARL SAGAN (B. 1934), U.S. ASTRONOMER

He who learns to remold the heart's desire, and not the mind's intent alone, will hold in his hands the key to our salvation.

EDMUND W. SINNOTT (1888–1968)
U.S. BIOLOGIST

ANIMAL KINSHIP

Ants are so much like human beings as to be an embarrassment. They farm fungi, raise aphids as livestock, launch armies into wars, use chemical sprays to alarm and confuse enemies, capture slaves. The families of weaver ants engage in child labor, holding their larvae like shuttles to spin out the thread that sews the leaves together for their fungus gardens. They exchange information ceaselessly. They do everything but watch television.

LEWIS THOMAS (1913–1993), U.S. BIOLOGIST

Turtles cough, burp, whistle, grunt and hiss, and produce social judgments. . . .

EDWARD HOAGLAND (B. 1932), U.S. ZOOLOGIST

It makes for a realization of the unity of organic nature to disclose in creatures which will pass through
the eye of a needle the presence of organs comparable to those in man himself.

SIR J. ARTHUR THOMSON (1861–1933)
SCOTTISH BIOLOGIST

No other explanation has ever been given of the
marvellous fact that the embryos of a man, dog, seal,
bat, reptile, etc. can at first hardly be distinguished
from each other.

CHARLES DARWIN (1809–1882)
BRITISH BIOLOGIST

Scientists who work on animal behavior are occupa-
tionally obliged to live chancier lives than most of
their colleagues, always at risk of being fooled by the
animals they are studying, or, worse, fooling themselves. Whether their experiments involve domesti-
cated laboratory animals or wild creatures in the
field, there is no end to the surprises that an animal
can think up in the presence of an investigator.

LEWIS THOMAS (1913–1993), U.S. BIOLOGIST

He was wont to say that man was but a great mischievous baboon.

ATTRIBUTED TO WILLIAM HARVEY (1578–1657)
BRITISH ANATOMIST

He who regrets with scorn that the shape of his own
canines, and their occasional great development in

other men, are due to our early forefathers having been provided with these formidable weapons, will probably reveal, by sneering, the line of his descent.

CHARLES DARWIN (1809–1882)
BRITISH BIOLOGIST

THE ART OF LIVING

Life is short, art long, opportunity fugitive, experimenting dangerous, reasoning difficult. . . . To do nothing is sometimes a good remedy.

HIPPOCRATES (460–400 B.C.)
GREEK, "FATHER OF MEDICINE"

If "A" equals success, then the formula is "A" equals "x" plus "Y" and "z," with "x" being work, "Y" play, and "z" keeping your mouth shut.

ALBERT EINSTEIN (1879–1955)
SWISS-AMERICAN PHYSICIST

When down in the mouth, remember Jonah: he came out all right.

THOMAS ALVA EDISON (1847–1931)
U.S. SCIENTIST

Put your regretter on zero.

MERVYN HINE, BRITISH PHYSICIST

A wise man ought to realize that health is his most valuable possession and learn how to treat his illnesses by his own judgement.

HIPPOCRATES (460–400 B.C.)
GREEK, "FATHER OF MEDICINE"

A man is sane morally at 30, rich mentally at 40, wise spiritually at 50 — or never.

SIR WILLIAM OSLER (1849–1919)
CANADIAN RESEARCH SCIENTIST

To violate the welfare of another person, as by lying to him, stealing from him, or taking away his life, is completely to prevent the attainment of those highest satisfactions which experience has shown can come only if we have affection for our fellow men and treat them as we would ourselves be treated.

EDMUND W. SINNOTT (1888–1968)
U.S. BIOLOGIST

I must admit that I personally measure success in terms of the contributions an individual makes to her or his fellow human beings.

MARGARET MEAD (1901–1978)
U.S. ANTHROPOLOGIST

There are three ideas which seem to me to stand out above all others in the influence they have exerted ... upon the development of the human race.... They are the following: (1) The idea of the Golden Rule; (2) The idea of natural law; (3) The idea of age-long growth, or evolution.

ROBERT MILLIKAN (1868–1953)
U.S. PHYSICIST

Virtue must grow inwardly.... Men have been forced to do right and taught what is right to do. Neither means has proven a complete success, nor ever will, I fear, unless their service is supplemented by an elevation of men's motives.

EDMUND W. SINNOTT (1888–1968)
U.S. BIOLOGIST

I don't know what your destiny will be, but one thing I do know: The only ones among you who will be really happy are those who will have sought and found how to serve.

ALBERT SCHWEITZER (1875–1965)
ALSATIAN-BORN MEDICAL MISSIONARY

Show me a thoroughly satisfied man and I will show you a failure.

THOMAS ALVA EDISON (1847–1931)
U.S. SCIENTIST

Constancy and conservatism are qualities of the lifeless, not the living.

EDMUND W. SINNOTT (1888–1968)
U.S. BIOLOGIST

Every great and deep difficulty bears in itself its own solution. It forces us to change our thinking in order to find it.

NIELS BOHR (1885–1962), DANISH PHYSICIST

I will have nothing to do with Absolutes, including absolute truth, absolute morality, absolute perfection and absolute authority.

JULIAN HUXLEY (1887–1975)
BRITISH ZOOLOGIST

I listen from within.

THOMAS ALVA EDISON (1847–1931)
U.S. SCIENTIST

I live in that solitude which is painful in youth, but delicious in the years of maturity.

ALBERT EINSTEIN (1879–1955)
SWISS-AMERICAN PHYSICIST

About the Editor

Shirley A. Jones has a bachelors degree in biology with a chemistry minor and a masters degree in English, Teaching of Writing.

Her experiences in the field of science are as varied as her interests. They include work in a herbarium, quality-control testing in a dairy-products laboratory, toxicity testing of pond liners for a fish hatchery, and a feasibility study on growing truffles symbiotically with filbert trees.

She has taught college writing classes and is herself a writer. She has had two science books published as well as a history book chronicling the process of invention.

Currently, she is conducting writing workshops that incorporate her science background.

She lives in Stockton, California with her husband.

Bibliographic Index

The Classic Wisdom Collection

If you would like a catalog of our fine books and cassettes, contact:

New World Library
58 Paul Drive
San Rafael, California 94903
(415) 472-2100

Or call toll-free: (800) 227-3900